CONFEDERATES

IN MONTANA TERRITORY

IN THE SHADOW OF PRICE'S ARMY

Ken Robison

THE
History
PRESS

Published by The History Press
Charleston, SC 29403
www.historypress.net

First published 2014

Manufactured in the United States

ISBN 978.1.62619.603.2

Library of Congress CIP data applied for.

Many histories of the Civil War record the exploits of the "big guys." Here's to the gray and the blue; the men, women and children from South and North who came to Montana Territory to find shelter, hope and opportunity; and the modern generations who treasure their past.

CONTENTS

FOREWORD

From Texas to Maine, from Minnesota to Florida, the nation engaged in an epic struggle of the War Between the States, the Civil War. The West, including the territory of Montana, has often been described as the relief valve for the great pressure cooker of the Civil War. Certainly the discovery of gold had a great deal to do with the sudden rush of people to the region, and the order or disorder of politics was to keep pace with this influx.

Territorial appointments such as first governor Sidney Edgerton were naturally Republican, and this generated a small but very active and vocal Republican presence in the territory. Another important component was that of the Union or War Democrats. But it was the third group that was to have the most profound effect on politics in the new territory. Southern Democrats had come into the territory in large numbers.

For years, historians have focused on this influx of Southern Democrats in Montana Territory and have pondered the reasons why they came in such large numbers. In a five-month period, from December 24, 1860, to May 21, 1861, eleven states left the Union to create the Confederate States of America. While this drama was playing itself out, the Lincoln administration was pulling out all stops in an effort to keep the border states of Maryland, Kentucky and Missouri in the Union. If the future had been left in the hands of their population, there is little doubt that these states would have followed their brethren into the new confederation. They were kept in the Union by military force. We know that of the three, Lincoln saw Missouri as the lynch pin. There was bitter fighting in Missouri in both the early and late stages of the war, and this led to the displacement of large numbers of people.

In July 1861, in the immediate aftermath of the Federal defeat at First Manassas (First Bull Run), President Lincoln ordered that Union forces in the war's western theater go on the offensive, "giving special attention to Missouri."

If one looks at a map of the country, it is evident why the state of Missouri was to be such a focus for either the preservation of the Union or the establishment of the Confederacy. All major trails that led to the West started in Missouri—the California Trail, the Oregon Trail and Santa Fe Trail. California had been admitted to the Union in 1859 and was surrounded by territories. There was a real and legitimate fear that it could be cut off and isolated with the loss of Missouri. Other factors that made the state so important were the tremendous gold strikes in far-off Idaho Territory, soon to become Montana Territory, plus the fact that all three of the major rivers—the Mississippi, the Missouri and the Ohio—critically important shipping arteries, went through or bordered the state. Control of the Mississippi River was strategically, economically and psychologically vital to both sides.

The first U.S. census of Montana Territory did not occur until 1870, by which time a major shift in the population had already taken place and certainly the population was in decline. In 1870, the total population of the territory was placed at 20,595, while it is likely that in the period 1864–66, the population might have hovered close to 30,000 centered in the gold camps. That Missouri contributed a significant number to that population is without doubt, although it is impossible to give an exact number. And these Missourians reflected a large number of the Southern Democrats to be found in the territory.

It has often been said that Missouri was kept in the Union on the point of Federal bayonets and that the extraordinary wartime powers of the Lincoln administration were well reflected there. With the suspension of the writ of habeas corpus, an untold number of pro-secession Missourians were simply detained as virtual prisoners of war and, when released, ordered out of the state, instructed to proceed to a western territory and remain there for the duration of the conflict. Another factor was the soldiers who had been captured, released and then exiled from the state with the same understanding that they not return until war's end. This situation was reflected in the population trend in Montana Territory; in the immediate aftermath of the war, many did return to their homes, while others did not. This mixture of exiled and displaced Missourians, civilians as well as former

Confederate soldiers added to the mix of Southern Democrats found in Montana Territory.

The impact of the proud and strong Southern people in the territorial days of Montana was a true reflection of the Southern character. Never give up. Never give in. It has been said that politically the Southern people have known nothing but defeat, and in many respects, this is true. But what is far more important is that the Southerner always comes back and rises to fight again. Never give up. Never give in.

Richard L. Thoroughman
Sons of Confederate Veterans

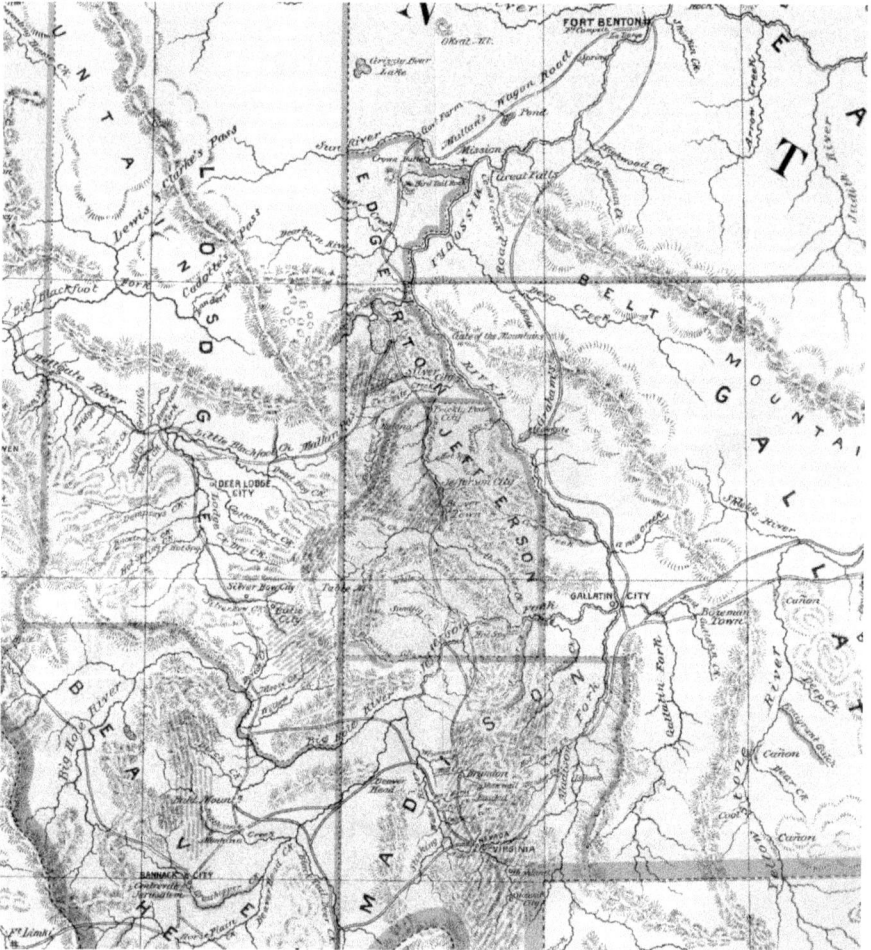

Map of Montana from Fort Benton to the gold mining camps of Bannack and Virginia City, 1865. *Author's collection.*

ACKNOWLEDGEMENTS

The response around Montana and the nation to my first Civil War book, *Montana Territory and the Civil War: A Frontier Forged on the Battlefield*, has been exciting. Much interest stems from the 150th anniversary of the Civil War and from the celebration of the creation of Montana Territory on May 26, 1864. Perhaps more interest comes from Montanans who have Civil War ancestors, many having inherited "treasures" from their Yankee or Rebel heritage.

From Missoula to Sidney, from Great Falls and Helena to Billings, libraries, bookstores and other venues have welcomed me to hold conversations and signings. Montana's independent booksellers like Fact and Fiction and Montana Book Company, though all too few, are treasures in our communities. To all booksellers, remember that eBooks are fun, but real books are keepsakes! Who has heard of a prized possession first-edition eBook?

To descendants of those who served in the Civil War who have protected and shared the diaries, letters, papers and artifacts handed down to them, exemplified by the Raymond Howard—Charlene Nava family, my admiration. To those active in reenactment groups, like Colonel Thomas Huether and his 1st U.S. Volunteer Infantry (the famed Galvanized Yankees), Tiea Toby (Clara Barton) and Jim Vaughn, keep up your great work. For encouragement and research assistance throughout, a special thanks to friend Dick Thoroughman of Fort Shaw, a descendant of Confederates Oliver H.P. Thoroughman and Colonel Thomas Thoroughman. To Jay

Hoar, my admiration for your knowledge of Civil War veterans, North and South. And to dear Kay Strombo of the Mineral County Museum, who shared her research of more than 6,200 Montana Civil War veterans.

To Kathy Mora, Jude Smith and their Great Falls Public Library for working with me to present the two-month series Civil War 150 to well over one thousand Civil War buffs with nine public events, including three reenactments. To Bob Harris, who is always with me in projects related to black history. To Reverend Phil Caldwell and his Mount Olive Christian Fellowship Choir and to Frank and Mary Ghee and Kathy Reed of Union Bethel A.M.E. Church for joining our special evening "Black Heritage and the Civil War." And to Rich Aarstad, Bill Rossiter, Aaron Parrett, Benjamin Donnely and Oliver Pflugg for bringing the Civil War to many.

To Aaron Flint of Northern Broadcasting Network for stimulating statewide interest in the Civil War by inviting me to join Voices of Montana and by broadcasting from Great Falls during our exciting Civil War 150 program.

The Montana Historical Society's Research Center and Photo Archives, led by Brian Shovers and Lory Morrow and all their staff, make every visit a pleasant adventure of discovery—many thanks. The Great Falls Public Library and The History Museum provide great environments in which to work. Our Overholser Historical Research Center reveals many research treasures, such as the diary of Private John Lilly, used in this book. Janet Thomson, Dennis Sugden and all my friends at the Great Falls Genealogy Society keep finding great research sources.

My thanks to the *Fort Benton River Press* and *Great Falls Tribune* for sharing my Civil War stories with the public, and my thanks to the many readers who have encouraged me to continue the series.

My appreciation to The History Press and editors Will McKay and Will Collicott for their skill and professionalism in bringing my Montana Civil War books into print.

Thanks to Karin and Ian Deal for being there to help with photos and graphic design, proofing and indexing. And to my wife, Michele, who tolerates my research piles and shares my love of history.

INTRODUCTION

To write about the Civil War is to step onto hallowed ground. As our nation continues to commemorate the 150th anniversary of the Civil War, many ask, "What role did Confederates and their sympathizers play in settling Montana Territory?" A legend persists that Montana was settled by "the left wing of Price's army"—meaning that Missourians came west in large numbers after defeats suffered by Major General Sterling Price's Confederate army. Most agree that pro-Confederate sentiment was strong as Montana's gold rush camps sprang into life and Montana Territory was created on May 26, 1864. But how strong was pro-Confederate presence and sentiment? Was it more than defecting and disillusioned men who abruptly left the service of General Price's Missouri State Guard when they suffered defeats in the western theater? How did this Southern sentiment influence politics in the new territory on the remote Upper Missouri region? What kind of men, women and children composed this influx of Southerners and sympathizers? Where did they come from? Why did they come? What impact did they have on Montana Territory?

Some clues came in my book *Montana Territory and the Civil War: A Frontier Forged on the Battlefield*. The gold strikes of 1862 and 1863 triggered a flood of those who sought fortune or opportunity, stampeding to rapidly forming mining camps over long overland wagon trails or the seasonal steamboat route up the Missouri River to the head of navigation at Fort Benton. Men and families from South and North migrated to the camps, where they brought their wartime experiences and strong sentiments with them.

Typical of the Southerners who came was Captain Nick Wall, exiled to the Upper Missouri as a condition of his parole after his capture at Camp Jackson near St. Louis in May 1861. Wall left politics behind as he began his new life building the largest and most sophisticated business enterprise in the new territory, integrating steamboat operations with overland freighting and retail merchandising.

Antagonism between South and North, between Confederate and Union sympathizers, ran deep, yet no pitched battles were fought in the rough streets of the mining towns. Rather, political strife and rhetoric took the place of armed warfare. Confederate sentiment was strong throughout the territory, especially in Madison County along the mining camps of Alder Gulch. Names reflected early sentiment: Dixie Town, Jeff Davis Gulch and an attempt to name the largest camp "Varina" to honor the wife of Confederate president Jefferson Davis. The compromise name became "Virginia City."

Confederate veterans were in on discovery of most of the largest strikes, including Georgians at Last Chance Gulch and secessionists who struck gold and named Confederate Gulch. Songs "Dixie" and "Bonnie Blue Flag" were on the "hit parade" in the hurdy-gurdy dance halls of Virginia City, and the assassination of President Abraham Lincoln was cheered and celebrated on the streets. When ex-Confederate soldiers formed Gallatin Masonic Lodge No. 6 in October 1866, they refused admission to African Americans, which was not surprising, but they also refused to admit whites who had fought for or supported the Union.

While it might have been lost in the East, the Civil War was won in the western theater as the Union seized control of the Mississippi River and saw Ulysses S. Grant emerge from obscurity to craft victories from Fort Donelson to Vicksburg, gaining control of the vital transportation corridor while carving the Confederacy into two regions.

Confederate soldiers and sympathizers flocked to Montana Territory during and after the war. Many of these men and their families came from Missouri and other border states after the defeat of General Price's Missouri State Guard. The secessionist influence was so strong in Montana that it remained a force in politics and the court of public opinion for many decades.

Look at a sampling of the colorful characters that came to the Montana frontier and hear their stories of the war, the environment in the battleground states and their way west. Confederate military leaders as well as common soldiers and their families sought shelter and opportunity on the remote mining frontier that became Montana.

The story begins with a look at their origins and ends with a discussion of the persistence of their "Lost Cause" as they arrived in Montana. In between, meet fascinating characters who came to Big Sky country, including guerrillas who fought with William Quantrill and "Bloody Bill" Anderson, as well as cavalrymen who rode with Confederate legends General Nathan Bedford Forrest and Colonel John S. Mosby. Their stories include key elements: where they came from, why they fought for the South, what they did during the war and why they came to Montana Territory.

Henry Kennerly first came to the Upper Missouri in 1855 with an Indian Peace Commission. He returned to his native Missouri to join his brothers to fight for the Confederacy. Before the end of the war, Kennerly returned to the Upper Missouri to work in the bison robe trade and become active in Democratic politics. Captain John H. Rogers, another Confederate soldier, also became active in Montana territorial politics. Elected to the first Montana legislature, Rogers triggered a firestorm of controversy when he refused to sign an "Ironclad Oath" of allegiance to the Union.

Colonel Thomas Thoroughman served in the Missouri State Guard before being captured by Union forces, paroled and banished to the western territories. Thoroughman became active in Democratic Party politics and was elected to Montana's first constitutional convention. A brilliant lawyer and politician, Thoroughman typified the many pro-secession Missourians who left Montana to return from exile to their home states before the 1870 U.S. Census. Although hard to measure, thousands of Southern-leaning men and their families returned to their home states in the years after the Civil War as political conditions settled and the Democratic Party regained control of the border and Southern states.

Nine-year-old Horace R. Buck from a Unionist family in Mississippi lived with his mother throughout the long siege of Vicksburg in the spring of 1863, when that critical Southern stronghold fell to the Union. After studying at Yale University, young Buck came up the Missouri River to Montana Territory to become a highly respected lawyer and rise to the top of his profession.

German immigrant John C. Lilly joined Colonel Nathan Bedford Forrest's 1st Kentucky Cavalry at the beginning of the war. Young Lilly rode alongside that brilliant, innovative cavalry officer, all the while recording his observations of life in the Kentucky Cavalry, his commander and their many engagements. Presented in this volume are many of Lilly's diary entries from his handwritten account, featuring everything from the thrill of victory in the early years to the agony of defeat as the long war progressed. Lilly's diary concludes with a tribute to his hero: "There never was a man in that war as a General that done any more daring deeds and hard fighting then General N.B. Forrest of the Confederate Army." At war's end, Lilly came up the Missouri River to Fort Benton, where he quickly established a reputation as one of the toughest, most colorful characters in a frontier filled with war veterans, adventurers and desperadoes. Whether running dance halls in the "Bloodiest Block in the West" or fighting the Nez Perce with Donnelly's Mounted Civilian Volunteers, John Lilly left an indelible mark on frontier Montana.

The names of William Clarke Quantrill, his Raiders and "Bloody Bill" Anderson are the stuff of legend, personifying the toughest of the unconventional guerrilla units in the border states throughout the Civil War. Riding with Quantrill, and at times with Anderson, were the three Berry boys: Ike, Richard and James. The latter, Jim Berry, left the battlefields to come to the mining camps of Montana Territory. After the war, he returned to Missouri with his family and joined the Sam Bass outlaw gang in the Black Hills gold rush to become active in stage and train robberies. Details of Jim Berry's life of crime, culminating in his shoot-out with a sheriff, make for gripping reading. His family descendants remain in Montana today.

Slaveholder Colonel James Conrad of the Shenandoah Valley of Virginia and his two young sons joined the Confederate army. The teenage boys, William G. and Charles E. Conrad, joined Colonel John S. Mosby's Rangers for the last year of the war. Mosby, refusing to surrender, disbanded his cavalry, and the Conrad boys returned to their devastated family plantation. They soon boarded a steamboat bound up the Missouri River, where they both became giants in Montana Territory.

The Moore brothers, Perry and John, left their Missouri home to fight for the Confederacy with both Missouri and Kentucky units. With the 9th Kentucky Cavalry in General John Hunt Morgan's division, the Moores served as military escorts in the final days before Confederate president Jefferson Davis surrendered. Returning home to northeastern Missouri, the brothers learned that their mother and younger siblings had departed for the western territories. The Moores searched the West to find their family.

Shirley C. Ashby left his home in the Shenandoah Valley to join the 1st/6th Virginia Cavalry. The fighting 6th fought in a staggering two hundred engagements throughout the war, and when General Robert E. Lee surrendered the Army of Northern Virginia in April 1865, the 6th Virginia Cavalry slipped through Union lines and later disbanded. Heading west, Ashby boarded a steamboat early in 1867. At Fort Benton, he worked for the Conrad brothers and made and lost fortunes on the frontier.

Raised in Virginia's Piedmont, Frank D. "Sandbar" Brown served in the Richmond Battalion before transferring to the Confederate War Department to act as orderly for his cousin Secretary of War James A. Seddon. Brown's stint in the war ended in the Confederate marines, and he headed up the Missouri River, working in the fur/bison robe trade. An unreconstructed Confederate, Brown settled in the Philipsburg mining area and assumed a leading role in the United Confederate Veterans.

Born a slave, Joseph Wells accompanied his master into the Missouri State Guard. Thousands of slaves went to war with the Confederate army as construction workers, teamsters and manservants. This manpower significantly helped the Confederacy, although most slaves were not armed and enlisted into the army until late in the war. At war's end, Joe Wells headed west, mining in Colorado and the Black Hills and holding various jobs in Montana Territory. Interviews in his elder years shed light on his fascinating life and raise puzzling questions.

Perhaps the most intriguing story, mixing Quantrill guerrillas, a battered steamboat, a teenage traveler, a charming murderer and a faded grave marker, is the saga of Langford "Farmer" Peel. The steamboat *Richmond* steamed up the Missouri River on a mission of revenge. This strange voyage with a colorful crew on their mission of vengeance makes this a saga to remember.

These stories reveal varied backgrounds, wartime experiences, motivations for migrating west and degrees of success and failure in finding hope and opportunity. Although economic status and attitudes toward slavery varied, most were motivated by greater loyalty to their state, considered by many to be their "country," rather than to the Union. Some were slave owners, while others had mixed feelings about the "peculiar institution." Yet all believed the rebellion was an issue of states' rights, not the abolition of slavery. Theirs was a War of Southern Independence, and for that, most were ready to fight.

Once Confederates and Southern sympathizers arrived in Montana, some quietly hid their past allegiances, while many mellowed over the years. Others were unrepentant throughout their lives, even passing it on to descendants. Over the decades, large-scale migration of Northerners and foreign immigrants further diluted Confederate fervor. Yet the Lost Cause persisted in Montana for many decades.

Chapter 1

FROM THE BATTLEFIELDS
OF THE WAR OF SOUTHERN
INDEPENDENCE

CONFEDERATE VETERANS SETTLE MONTANA

Thousands of men who fought under the Bonnie Blue Flag came west during and after the awful struggle and established themselves in what was then a rugged frontier. Arriving in newly formed Montana Territory, these men, women and children joined families arriving from the North and from abroad, as well as thousands of Native Americans who had lived in the region for centuries.

Fort Benton, the fur/robe trade center on the Missouri River, had long been a multiracial melting pot. In the opinion of historian J.W. Smurr, Fort Benton "was practically an appendage of the state of Missouri and had long been the headquarters of Missourians associated with the fur trade."

With the gold strikes in Alder Gulch and the major defeats of Major General Sterling Price and the Missouri State Guard in 1862 and 1864, thousands flocked to newly formed Madison County. Almost everyone attributed this early migration to Union domination of Missouri. Many secessionist Missourians, whether in Confederate service or not, left their homes and moved west. Some came as exiles, paroled to the western territories; others as deserters or draft evaders. Some came after service and discharge. Families came to avoid the insurgency fighting all around them; others for opportunity after their slaves had been freed and their plantations destroyed. The western territories became a safety valve for a wartime population on the move. Even remote Montana Territory could not escape the effect of the Civil War.

The first territorial census hurriedly taken in Montana in September 1864 recorded 15,812 nonnative residents—regrettably, neither place of birth

Sterling "Old Pap" Price, legendary commander of Confederate forces in Missouri. *Library of Congress.*

nor former residence was recorded. Three-quarters of these early transient miners were found in the mining camps of Madison County in southwestern Montana. Over the next two years, many of these miners stampeded on to new gold strikes in Last Chance, Confederate and other gulches. During these years, many thousands more arrived in this land of opportunity, some with and some without families. The population of the new territory might have grown to thirty thousand by the mid-1860s, unrecorded by any census.

During 1864–65, as the new territory was forming, it is likely that perhaps half of the residents were pro-secession, whether in Confederate service or sentiment. In addition, the Northern contingent included many Peace Democrats or Copperheads, those who wanted peace with the South at any price.

Both foreign-born and native-born residents included large numbers of Irish, many of whom were loyal to the Union, yet almost all of these War Democrats voted democratic. Thus, Missourians, Southerners, Copperheads and Irish formed an uneasy coalition to make the Democratic Party dominant for several decades. Just how uneasy is indicated by the feelings of territorial secretary Thomas Francis Meagher when he complained, "These sympathizers with the Rebellion acquired not only a strong majority in the territorial legislature, but the mastery, moreover, of the political action of the territory." Meagher later tempered his rhetoric to cultivate the Southern vote.

In fact, Missourians and Irish controlled the Democratic Party, and if the nominations were divided correctly, there was a semblance of harmony. Put another way, the Irish and Missourians "hated each other pretty cordially, but as fall approached there was some flirtation between them."

Another measure of the influence of Missourians in Montana Territory is the composition of Confederates present. Of 450 identified Confederate veterans in Montana, almost half (47.2 percent) were Missourians who fought for the Confederacy. Some 65 percent were from the border states of Missouri, Kentucky, Arkansas and Tennessee. Soldiers from the Deep South and Virginia each comprised 13 percent. In addition, many of those soldiers fighting for the South in the border states were Virginia born.

The early legislatures in Montana Territory had a strong Southern influence. This led to incidents like the adoption of a bill by the 1866 Legislative Council that prohibited "Negroes and mulattos" from testifying in cases involving white parties. On reflection, council reversed its decision the following day. The legislature passed a school law effective in 1872 that paved the way for "separate but equal" schools for children of "African descent" at the discretion of school trustees. Battles were fought in Helena and Fort Benton over separate schools, rejecting them more because of added cost until the legislature repealed this discriminatory legislation in 1883. In Fort Benton, battles were fought over school segregation by dueling editorials in the Copperhead Democrat *Benton Record* and the Republican *River Press*.

By 1868, placer mines were playing out, causing a large-scale departure of discouraged miners and those who lived off the boom prosperity of the

Early tintype of unidentified Confederate soldiers in Montana Territory. *Author's collection.*

mining camps. In addition, thousands of Missourians and other Southerners departed from their wartime refuge to return to their home states or regions. This exodus caused a drastic drop in Montana's population to 20,595 by the first U.S. Census in 1870. That census showed that just 6 percent of the population had been born in Missouri and less than 10 percent in the border states. By then, about half of Montana's residents were Northern born and 28 percent foreign born.

By 1900, the Confederate veterans who had come as soldiers of the "Lost Cause" had become old-timers who were dwindling in numbers if not in passion. For many years, all political parties found it necessary to cater to the Southern men of Missouri, known in the Unionist *Montana Post* as the "left wing of Price's army." They were Rebels then, but by the time Montana became a state in 1889, most had become loyal citizens.

Many Confederates, such as William and Charles Conrad and Shirley Ashby, became prominent in the business and political life of the territory. It took some of them many years to become reconciled to the fact that they had been whipped, and there were many mining camps where, for years, it was popular to cheer for Jeff Davis and General Robert E. Lee while singing songs of the South. However, unreconstructed Rebels would often fraternize with the blue-coated men from the North, except at election time, when discussions became hostile and heated.

The first Montana delegate to the U.S. Congress was Irish-American James Cavanagh, and while he was an exceptional man and a splendid orator, he did not suit the Missourians, and he was turned down in the democratic convention after two terms. For the first time in the young territory, the Republicans took advantage of the fight between the Missourians and the Irish and nominated their most brilliant orator, William H. Claggett. After Claggett's one term as delegate, the Democrats reunited to select Minnesota war veteran Martin Maginnis, and the Irishman was an easy victor.

Despite the large number of Confederate veterans in Montana in the early days, their veterans' organization, the United Confederate Veterans (UCV), did not organize until 1898. It then expanded rapidly to thirteen camps with some 176 members. The UCV in Montana largely resulted from the energy of Frank D. Brown of Philipsburg, a gold miner, farmer and businessman who served many years as major general, commanding the Northwest Division of the United Confederate Veterans.

Ironically, the first U.S. Army soldiers stationed in Montana Territory were ex-Confederates. These were Confederates captured by Union forces who chose to enlist in 1864 for frontier service rather than remain in the overcrowded prisoner of war camp at Fort Lookout, Maryland. The first regiment was designated the 1st U.S. Volunteer Infantry, known as "Galvanized Yankees," with ex-Confederate soldiers and Union officers. According to the newspaper *Frontier Scout*, published in 1865 by the 1st U.S.

Jefferson Davis, president of the Confederate States of America. *Library of Congress.*

Opposite: First U.S. Volunteer Infantry (Galvanized Yankees) in camp at Fort Benton, 1865. Pen-and-ink sketch by David Parchen. *Overholser Historical Research Center.*

Volunteers, before each man enlisted, he was separately questioned and given four alternatives: he could be exchanged or paroled, head north to work on government fortifications, remain in prison or enlist as a Union soldier. No coercion was used—it was an act of free will. There were no reservations or promises made that they would not be sent to the front to engage in deadly conflict with their Southern friends. Without delay, they shouldered their muskets and donned their equipment, ready to go wherever their country called. Many laid down their lives, dying from disease or during combat with Indians, and with but few exceptions, they served loyally.

Four companies with six hundred ex-Confederate soldiers came up the Missouri River to Fort Rice, Dakota Territory. On May 12, 1865, First Lieutenant Horace S. Hutchins of Company H, 1st U.S. Volunteers, and nine men embarked the steamboat *Deer Lodge*, under orders from their commander, Colonel Charles Dimon, "to control the trade with Indians between [Fort Benton] and Fort Union." The *Deer Lodge* arrived at Fort Benton on May 30, and the soldiers remained during the summer to provide transportation security. These Galvanized Yankees were the first U.S. Army soldiers stationed in Montana Territory.

Five days prior to the army's arrival at Fort Benton, ten woodcutters nearby had been killed by Kainai Blackfoot led by war chief Calf Shirt.

The first steamboat arrival, on May 28, 1865, was the American Fur Company's steamer *Yellowstone*. Historian Joel Overholser described tensions on the Missouri River as the Civil War neared its end and the *Yellowstone* made its way upriver:

Charles Chouteau and the new owners of the trading post at Fort Benton [Hubbell and Hawley] *were aboard. There was the almost routine sniping by hostile Sioux. At old Fort Sully (present Pierre) passengers heard the news of Lincoln's assassination, and when the* Yellowstone *reached Fort Rice, Col. Charles Dimon met the boat and placed the whole party under arrest for "jubilating over" Lincoln's death. Dimon then threatened to have Chouteau shot for his assumed Confederate sympathies...Intervention by Northerners Hubbell and Hawley resulted in Dimon's giving up on his firing squad. As Dimon's command was of ex-Confederate soldiers...one might wonder about their willingness to carry out any firing squad service.*

Chapter 2

FROM THE UPPER MISSOURI
TO CIVIL WAR MISSOURI

Private Henry Kennerly

When the Civil War erupted in April 1861, the Upper Missouri region that became Montana was a vast land of many cultures. In addition to the thousands of Native Americans populating the dozen tribes, a small number of white Americans, Canadians, French, Metis, Spanish and Mexicans were present, primarily involved in the fur and robe trade.

One of the Americans on the Upper Missouri in 1861 was Henry Atkinson Kennerly, who was born at Jefferson Barracks near St. Louis on December 2, 1835, the son of George H. and Alziere Menard Kennerly. Henry's father had served as a U.S. Army quartermaster general before becoming a prominent merchant in St. Louis, while his mother came from the fur trading Menard family, related through marriage to explorer William Clark. The Kennerlys were friends of another important fur trade family, the Chouteaus.

Nineteen-year-old Henry Kennerly first came to the Upper Missouri in 1855 as a private secretary and clerk for senior Indian commissioner Alfred Cumming, as Cumming and Governor Isaac I. Stevens of Washington Territory negotiated a treaty with the Blackfoot, Gros Ventre, Flathead and Nez Perce nations. This Treaty of 1855 began a new era for native Indian–American relations in the Upper Missouri region. The treaty council culminated American efforts to impose their own brand of peace and order among the Indian nations along both the east and west slopes of the northern Rocky Mountains.

Commissioner Cumming and his party departed St. Louis on June 6, 1855, on the steamboat *St. Mary*, commencing the long trip up the Missouri

A scene at the Blackfeet Treaty Council of 1855, where Kennerly served as secretary for Commissioner Cumming. *Library of Congress.*

River. Accompanying Cumming were Kennerly; Charles P. Chouteau, son of Pierre Chouteau Jr. and director of operations for the American Fur Company; and Major Alexander Culbertson, supervisor of company operations on the Upper Missouri. *St. Mary* also carried company trade goods, as well as government treaty annuities for the various tribes. In this early steamboat era, goods were off-loaded at Fort Union to proceed laboriously upriver to Fort Benton by mackinaw boats.

The Cumming party proceeded from Fort Union along the Northern Overland Wagon Road, arriving at Fort Benton on August 19. There, couriers were dispatched to summon the tribes to treaty council. Kennerly, with guide, was detailed to search for the tribes of the Blackfoot Nation, including Chiefs Little Dog and Lame Bull. The council finally convened near the mouth of the Judith River on October 16, and the Lame Bull Treaty was concluded, while the distribution of presents and annuities continued until October 20. Two days later, Cumming and Kennerly departed downriver to St. Louis.

In the spring of 1856, Kennerly again ascended the Missouri to Fort Benton, this time employed by the American Fur Company. In the fall of that year, he descended the Missouri to northern Nebraska Territory (later Dakota Territory). By late May 1857, a new fur trade coalition was formed in opposition to the American Fur Company. St. Louis merchant Robert

Campbell led this firm with Frost, Todd and Company. Daniel M. Frost and John Blair Todd established a trading post at Vermillion and hired Henry Kennerly to operate their post, which served both the army at Fort Randall and nearby Indian tribes. Kennerly was also named registrar of land with an office in Vermillion. There, Henry was reunited with his brother Lewis Hancock Kennerly, who also worked for Frost, Todd and Company.

As the dark clouds of the Civil War began to form in Missouri in 1859–60, both Frost and Lewis Kennerly returned to become leaders in the pro-secession Missouri Volunteer Militia. That brigade deployed to the Kansas border on the Southwest Expedition in November 1860 with both Lewis and his brother Samuel Kennerly in their ranks.

When the Civil War erupted in Missouri in May 1861 with the Camp Jackson Affair, Brigadier General Daniel M. Frost commanded the secessionist Missouri Volunteer Militia, which included Lewis and Samuel Kennerly, as well as their teenage brother, James Amadee Kennerly. After the surrender of the militia to Captain Nathaniel Lyon's loyal Union regiments on May 10, Frost and the three Kennerlys broke their paroles to join the Confederate-aligned Missouri State Guard under General Sterling Price.

Sam, Jim and Lew Kennerly all became commissioned officers in the 1st Missouri Infantry Regiment, one of the most effective units in Price's army. The 1st Missouri, composed largely of the young men who had been captured at Camp Jackson, fought in nine pitched battles, including Shiloh, Corinth, Tuscumbia Bridge, Altoona and Franklin. Commanding the 1st Missouri was Colonel John Stevens Bowen, married to Mary Kennerly, a sister of the Kennerly brothers.

Eighteen-year-old James Kennerly enlisted as a drummer boy but soon became bandmaster of the regimental band. He later commanded Company A. Following the Battle of Franklin (Tennessee) on November 30, 1864, one of Lieutenant Kennerly's men in Company A wrote of the tough fighting:

> Our appalling loss was not generally realized until the next morning, when a ghastly sight was revealed to those still living...Our regiment had but three officers left for duty, Capt. James Wickersham and Lieuts. James Kennerly and Patrick Collins. Our army was a wreck. Our comrades were lying in the embrace of death. So many young hearts were stilled forever which a few hours ago beat high in the prospect of soon being at home in Missouri.

Federal troops drilling at Camp Jackson, St. Louis, site of the first clash of the Civil War in Missouri, on May 10, 1861. *From* The Photographic History of the Civil War, *Vol. I.*

On April 9, 1865, Lieutenant James Kennerly and most his men of Company A were captured at the siege of Fort Blakely, Alabama. He was held at Ship Island, a desolate barrier island in the Gulf of Mexico, and at Parish Prison, New Orleans, before being paroled at the end of the war.

Lieutenant Lewis Kennerly of Company D served as adjutant for his brother-in-law, General Bowen. Lewis was severely wounded in the hip and thigh in the Peach Orchard at the Battle of Shiloh. Promoted to captain, he was wounded again a year later during the First Missouri

Brigade's action at Grand Gulf, Mississippi. Despite his wounds, Lewis was promoted to major, appointed judge advocate and assigned to staff duty until war's end.

Lieutenant Samuel Augustin Kennerly of Company C mustered in to the 1st Missouri Infantry at Memphis on June 22, 1861. He participated in battles at Shiloh, Corinth and Baker Creek, Mississippi, where on May 16, 1863, he was wounded and left for dead until found on the battlefield by his sister, Mary Kennerly Bowen. Captured by Union troops, Major General Ulysses Grant ordered the parole of 445 wounded Rebel soldiers, including

Sam Kennerly. Sam was promoted to captain and spent the next year in and out of military hospitals recuperating from his wounds. Rejoining the 1st Missouri, he took command of Company A in time for skirmishes at Lovejoy's Station, Clayton, Georgia, during Sherman's Atlanta Campaign. There, on September 5, the final day of fighting, he was killed and buried on the battlefield close to where he fell.

After John Bowen's capture at Camp Jackson, his wife, Mary, smuggled his unit's flag out of camp by wrapping it around her waist as a sash. He then broke parole to secure a commission as a Confederate colonel and raised the 1st Missouri Infantry Regiment. After being promoted to brigadier general, in March 1862, he was severely wounded at Shiloh. Recovering, Bowen took command of the First Missouri Brigade and distinguished himself early in the Vicksburg campaign. Promoted to major general, he fell gravely ill during the siege of Vicksburg and died nine days after the Confederate fortress surrendered on July 4, 1863. Wife Mary endured the long siege at

Steamboats
(right) at the Fort
Benton levee
during the early
years of overland
freighting.
*Overholser Historical
Research Center.*

Vicksburg to be with her husband and saved two battle flags from capture by hiding them in her husband's ambulance.

In September 1862, Henry Kennerly was elected to the Dakota territorial House of Representatives that met at Yankton on December 12. After adjournment of the legislature on January 9, 1863, Kennerly returned to St. Louis to join his three fighting brothers in the 1st Missouri Infantry. Little is known of Henry's service except that he served as a staff officer for at least one year and suffered a wound below the knee before accepting a medical discharge.

In the spring of 1864, Kennerly returned to the Upper Missouri. He disembarked on the Fort Benton levee, where he was engaged as a clerk for the American Fur Company until it sold out the following year.

The mid-1860s began the wild and wooly years at Fort Benton. Dozens of steamboats with vast quantities of cargo landed at the levee each summer. The rough streets of the town were roamed by the rich and famous, scoundrels and killers, fur and robe traders and their native wives and children, merchants and gamblers, Native Indians and wood hawks, discharged soldiers and draft evaders, Irish Fenians and exiled Metis and, eventually, white women and children. Henry Kennerly was in his element.

In November 1865, Acting Governor Thomas Francis Meagher and Gad Upson, Indian agent to the Blackfeet, arranged a peace treaty. Thousands of Blackfeet assembled at Fort Benton for the ceremony, camping out along the Fort Benton bottom. Two decades later, the *Fort Benton River Press* of December 24, 1884, gave this account of an escapade, typical of Fort Benton life in the early years:

A large train of the Diamond R transportation company was also camped on the flats. They had transported a four-pound howitzer on the back of a faithful mule from the steamer Shreveport *that had unloaded her cargo [downriver] at Cow Island. The howitzer had been left for the protection of the freight and came with the last of the supplies.*

The men in charge of the "little gun" conceived the idea of showing the immense congregation of Indians its strength by discharging it from the back of a mule. The howitzer, loaded with grapeshot, was securely fastened upon the back of a large, sleepy looking train mule with the muzzle pointed toward the tail, and the patient, unsuspecting animal was led to the bank of the river...and a target set up across the river. The rear of the mule was aligned with the target, and the train men, officers, curious old-timers, and wondering Indians were arranged in a semi-circle around the mule.

The appointed chief of ceremonies advanced and, when all was in readiness, inserted a time fuse in the touch-hole of the howitzer and then retired. In a short time the quiet, unruffled mule heard a fizzing just back of his ears, which made him uneasy, and he immediately began to turn his head to investigate. As he did so his body turned and the howitzer began to take in other points of the compass. The mule became more excited as his curiosity became more and more intense, and in a few seconds he had his four feet in a bunch, making more revolutions a minute than the bystanders dared to count...The train men and Indians scattered pell-mell over the flat toward the bluffs, running as if they thought that in flight lay their only safety, and that, too, at a rate of speed much greater than grapeshot. Judging from the alacrity with which Col. [Charles A.] Broadwater, H.A. Kennerly, Joe Healy and Mose Solomon slid over the bank of the river, they were not opposed to immersion; Matt Carroll, George Steell and James Arnoux sprinted toward the store; Hi Upham, John J. Healy and

Bill Hamilton began to throw up breastworks with their sheath knives, while I.G. Baker and one or two of the peace commissioners were turning back-springs toward the fort.

While the mule, with his heels in mid-air, was shaken with the most violent agitation, there was a puff of smoke, a thud, and the mule—oh, where was he? Ask of the winds, for not a soul saw him, and they will tell you a lonely, forlorn mule might have been seen turning over and over until he tumbled over the bank with his howitzer a cast anchor in the river. The shot went toward the fort, striking the figure of a buffalo [weather vane] *that was used as an advertisement at the fort, and which hung there until the last two or three years, and which many of the citizens of Fort Benton will remember was well perforated with balls. Further investigation has brought to light the fact that X. Beidler was the commander in chief elected, and that it was his first buffalo.* [X. Beidler being the famed vigilante hangman and U.S. marshal in the new territory.]

Henry Kennerly began as clerk and, over time, became trader, the agent for a succession of T.C. Power & Brother–owned trading posts in Blackfeet country. Tom C. Power and his younger brother John arrived on the Upper Missouri in 1867 to form a powerful trading company. Kennerly operated Power's Willow Rounds post on the Marias River. In 1872, Kennerly moved to Power's Fort Maginnis trading post on Badger Creek to capture more of the Canadian Blackfoot trade. About 1874, Kennerly married Mary Successful Kill, a Blackfoot woman, and raised their children: Bertia, Perry, Hattie, Agnes, Jerome and Sarah Wright (adopted). Kennerly remained at the Maginnis post until 1880.

From his arrival in Montana Territory, Henry Kennerly took an active interest in politics and was elected as a Democrat to the territorial House of Representatives for three terms (1867, 1869, 1880). He continued his political activities serving as Choteau County treasurer, assessor and sheriff. While holding county offices, Kennerly lived with his family on a ranch at the mouth of Kennerly Coulee on the Teton River, about thirty-five miles west of Fort Benton.

Later, Kennerly ranched on Birch Creek, a tributary of the Two Medicine River on the Blackfeet Reservation. In 1896, he remarried another Piegan woman, Marguerite "Neat-A-Sin-Ne" Blackweasel, daughter of (Old) Mountain Chief.

Kennerly keenly felt the responsibility to educate his children. In March 1890, he arrived in Great Falls with thirty-nine multiracial children from the Piegan

Henry Kennerly with other Fort Benton traders at Sioux City, 1866. *Standing left to right*: Mose Solomon, African American Bob Mills and John Largent. *Seated left to right*: Joe Kipp and Kennerly. *Overholser Historical Research Center*.

Agency, including his two eldest sons. He put the children on the eastbound train destined for Carlisle Indian Industrial School, the first native children to attend Carlisle from this region. Kennerly then placed his younger children at Holy Family Mission on the Two Medicine River on the reservation. To finance the education of his children, Kennerly secured a position as issue agent on the Blackfeet Reservation (1890–91), serving from the office at Piegan. From 1894 on, he served as deputy U.S. customs officer, stationed at the Blackfeet Agency, then just east of Browning, where he also operated a trading post.

By 1899, Kennerly had lost his eyesight, forcing him into retirement. A letter of April 22, 1899, reported to the *Great Falls Tribune*:

> *Henry A. Kennerly, well known throughout the state, now resides at Blackfoot station; he is totally blind but is enjoying good health. Mr. Kennerly is an old Confederate soldier who participated in several battles and was on the staff of one of the southern generals at the capture of Vicksburg, where General* [Ulysses] *Grant, upon seeing him, shook hands very cordially, as they were intimate friends before the war, the general having met his wife at the home of Mr. Kennerly's sister.* [Henry Kennerly's eldest sister, Eliza Clark Kennerly Stevenson, was one year younger than Julia Dent Grant, and the two were prominent in St. Louis society.]

The aging Henry Kennerly moved to the home of adopted daughter, Mrs. Sarah Wright Allison, in Cut Bank. The Allisons cared for Kennerly for more than a decade, and during the winter of 1912–13, they assisted him in recording his recollections of life on the Upper Missouri. Tragically, most of this manuscript later was destroyed by fire, with only his account of the Blackfeet Council of 1855 surviving.

On Tuesday, July 8, 1913, the old Confederate soldier, fur trader, legislator and pioneer on the Upper Missouri, Henry Atkinson Kennerly, died at the Allison home at the age of seventy-three.

Chapter 3

FROM PRICE'S ARMY TO
THE MONTANA LEGISLATURE

CAPTAIN JOHN H. ROGERS

Captain John H. Rogers left the battlefields of Missouri and brought his fight and honor with him to Montana Territory. The first territorial census taken in September 1864 found three-quarters of the 15,812 residents clustered along the mining camps of Alder Gulch in Madison County, a hotbed of secessionist sympathizers. The first election showed Madison County with an overwhelming Democratic vote, while Unionists carried the other counties. The Democrats in Madison County included large numbers of secessionist Democrats and some Peace Democrats or Copperheads, who advocated peace at any cost. Montana's Unionists included Republicans and some War Democrats, who supported the Union and the war but not necessarily President Lincoln and his Republican Congress. The first Montana territorial legislature was divided with the Council Unionist and the House Democratic, each by one vote.

When the first territorial legislature met on December 12 in a log cabin in Bannack, Governor Sidney Edgerton opened the verbal clash by denouncing the Confederacy in a fiery message to the legislature:

> *This unhallowed rebellion had its origin in the lust for power and the insane desire to extend and perpetuate human bondage. For years this conspiracy had been plotting, till at length, under the imbecile administration of James Buchanan, it threw off all disguise and assumed the defiant attitude of treason... The issue is fully made up between loyalty and treason; the opposing armies are in the field to decide the question by the wager of battle, and between them there is no middle ground.*

Montana's first territorial governor, Sidney
Edgerton. *Thomas Minkler Collection.*

As the legislature began to
organize, a second clash occurred.
The members of the House of
Representatives attempted to seat
one representative who refused
to swear to an "Ironclad Oath"
of allegiance to the United
States. That member was
Captain John H. Rogers, and
in the words of Joseph Kinsey
Howard in his legendary book
Montana: High, Wide, and Handsome,
"in his [Roger's] little gesture the
Confederacy fought a last battle for
the western Territories, and lost."

Governor Edgerton had prescribed
the "Ironclad Oath" for the territorial
legislature, similar to the oath then required
for members of Congress and for western territories. That oath required
Captain Rogers and other members to swear that they had never
voluntarily borne arms against the United States; this Rogers refused
to do. The oath was an attempt by congressional Radical Republicans
to preempt ex-Confederate soldiers from regaining political power. The
Rogers case escalated the war between the governor and the legislature
and led to bitter feelings.

Governor Edgerton notified the legislature there would be no further
communication until Rogers swore to the Ironclad Oath. Until then, the
governor would not recognize or address it, and any laws it attempted to pass
would be void. The governor further hinted that the legislature might receive
no pay. An attempt to break the deadlock with a new oath allowing Rogers to
swear allegiance to the United States without reference to past military service
failed to gain the governor's agreement, and Rogers was not admitted. Yet he
was reelected in 1866 and seated without incident—Governor Edgerton had
by then departed.

Out of these sharp clashes grew the claim that the governor was arbitrary
and dictatorial. The bitterness smoldered on until 1867, when the Third

Captain John H. Rogers fought for the South under General Sterling Price before being elected to the first Montana legislature. *Montana Historical Society 944-624.*

Legislature changed the name of Edgerton County to Lewis and Clark County. Then Speaker of the House John H. Rogers paid Governor Edgerton back and then some.

Captain John H. Rogers was a Missourian and, in fact, had been a former officer in General Price's army. He was one of those southerners Governor Edgerton had in mind when he excoriated the "traitors" in the territory, as he did bitterly in Montana's first election campaign.

John H. Rogers was born in Pittsylvania County, Virginia, on May 14, 1838. His parents, William B. and Sally Stone Rogers, moved to Jackson County, Missouri, in 1847, and he graduated with distinction from Bethany College in today's West Virginia in 1859.

In the spring of 1861, Rogers enlisted in the Missouri State Guard under General Sterling Price. He had joined the guard in response to Governor Claiborne Jackson's call for volunteers to oppose any armed force that might invade the state to upset its neutrality.

A natural leader, Rogers was in the fight at Wilson's Creek in southern Missouri on August 10, 1861, when Major General Price's army defeated Brigadier General Nathaniel Lyon's forces that included men from Iowa and Kansas, as well as Missouri. Captain Rogers also participated in the siege of Lexington, September 11–20, when General Price's troops routed the Union military force that had entrenched itself in the famous Masonic College there, just a few miles east of Rogers's home near Independence.

Captain Rogers drew the line when General Price decided later in the fall of 1861 to bring his Missouri State Guard formally into the Confederate army, then assembling in northwestern Arkansas. Rogers, willing to fight for Missouri but not for the Confederacy, resigned his commission and, in the spring of 1862, headed west.

Captain Rogers arrived in Alder Gulch in the early summer of 1863 just weeks after the discovery of gold by the Fairweather party. He came from the Colorado mining camps in a stampede of men who had heard of the earlier Bannack gold strikes. Some, like Rogers, already had seen service in the contending armies. Others were trying to escape conscription. Still more came with their families to escape the raids and pillaging by bushwhackers and jayhawkers in the early years of the war.

After his wartime service and his brief mining days in Colorado and Alder Gulch, Captain Rogers determined that the new territory would be his home. He helped organize the first school district in Madison County and served as director. Fellow Missourian Major John P. Bruce launched the *Montana Democrat* in Virginia City in the fall of 1865, and Rogers soon became its editor, winning recognition for his vigorous editorials advocating the Democratic Party. He married a Missouri-born woman, the daughter of Mr. and Mrs. Thomas H. Irvine, in 1867. The following year, he was admitted to the Montana bar and became editor and eventual owner of the *Independent* in Deer Lodge.

Finding an opportunity to become one of the first to develop the rich Pilgrim Bar in the Pioneer district northwest of Deer Lodge, Rogers sold the *Independent*. In the spring of 1870, he moved his family to Yamhill, where he began mining operations on a large scale. Two years later, he was elected for a third time to the territorial legislature and served as Speaker of the House in the 1873 and 1874 sessions.

Union general Nathaniel Lyon died at the Battle of Wilson Creek, an early victory for General Price. *Library of Congress.*

Tragedy struck on July 27, 1874, when Captain John H. Rogers was fatally injured in a runaway wagon accident on the hill descending into Yamhill. He died within a few hours, and the whole territory mourned. Just thirty-six years of age, Rogers had captured the hearts of all. Today, he rests in Saint Patrick's Cemetery in Butte.

Ten years after Governor Sidney Edgerton had denied Rebel Captain Rogers the right to sit in the territorial legislature, Montana's Republican leaders and veterans of the Grand Army of the Republic joined an overflow crowd in paying an emotional tribute as Episcopal bishop Daniel S. Tuttle ended his eulogy for Rogers: "Truly, an upright life has its reward!"

Chapter 4

FROM MISSOURI STATE GUARD TO MONTANA STATE MILITIA

COLONEL THOMAS THOROUGHMAN

Southerners exiled to Montana Territory during the Civil War wore their banishment as a badge of honor. Lieutenant Colonel Thomas Thoroughman, a Confederate soldier from Missouri, certainly did. In Montana, that qualified him to command the new territory's first militia.

Born in St. Joseph, Missouri, on Christmas Day 1832, Albert Thomas Thoroughman was the son of War of 1812 veteran Charles Thoroughman of disputed land between Virginia and Pennsylvania and Ruth Florea of Ohio. The Thoroughman family moved west to Ohio and then south to Buchanan County, northwestern Missouri.

Young Tom Thoroughman married Emily Ann Perkins, a native of Bracken County, Kentucky. They had three daughters—Ida, Lillie and Lou—before divorcing in 1866 through an act of the Montana legislature signed by Acting Governor Thomas Francis Meagher. Thoroughman was admitted to the Missouri bar in 1854 and practiced law with Alexander C. Davis, who remained his lifelong partner in war and peace. Thoroughman was appointed assistant city attorney of St. Joseph to fill an unexpired term. He then won election as city attorney and, in 1860, was elected to the office of circuit attorney for nine counties, including Buchanan. Earlier in 1860, he had run and been defeated for the Democratic Party nomination for Congress.

In the midst of Thoroughman's term of office, the Civil War broke out in Missouri with the Camp Jackson affair. His friend and law partner Alex Davis joined the Missouri State Guard under General Price and was commissioned lieutenant colonel in the Fifth Division early in the war. Davis

Lithographic image of Colonel Thomas Thoroughman, Missouri Rebel and Montana militia commander. *Author's collection.*

The Battle of Elkhorn Tavern (or Pea Ridge) in the spring of 1862 resulted in a disastrous defeat for General Price's Confederate forces. *Library of Congress.*

Major General Earl Van Dorn led the Confederate Army of the West in the decisive Battle of Elkhorn Tavern, which resulted in a Union victory. *Library of Congress*.

fought at Wilson's Creek on August 10, 1861, and at the First Battle of Lexington one month later.

Tom Thoroughman also sympathized with the cause of the Confederacy, and early in 1862, he accepted a commission as lieutenant colonel in the state guard, by then a part of the Confederate army. Lieutenant Colonel

Thoroughman served as paymaster and Alex Davis as judge advocate on the staff of Brigadier General Alexander C. Steen (and, later, Brigadier General James P. Saunders) in the Fifth Division, which was composed of recruits from Buchanan and other northwestern counties.

By early 1862, Union forces effectively forced the guard out of Missouri. The Union army under Brigadier General Samuel R. Curtis moved south from central Missouri, pushing Confederate forces into Arkansas. Major General Earl Van Dorn reorganized his forces as the Army of the West and prepared to launch a counteroffensive to recapture northern Arkansas and Missouri. The resulting Battle of Elkhorn Tavern (also known as Pea Ridge) was fought on March 7–8, five miles east of Pea Ridge in northwestern Arkansas.

General Curtis deployed 10,250 men, a balance of midwestern men and German immigrants, along strongly fortified defensive lines on the north bank of Little Sugar Creek. General Van Dorn planned to move his 16,000-man Army of the West, including Price's men, around the flanks to attack from the rear and cut off Union troops from their supply lines. In his haste to attack, fatally General Van Dorn left his own supply train with rations and bullets many hours in the rear. The Fifth Division, with the rest of General Price's Missourians, was assigned as the left wing of General Van Dorn's Army.

During March 7, the first day of the battle, Curtis's forces held off the Confederate attack and on the second day drove them from the field. This decisive battle was the largest of the Civil War fought west of the Mississippi, with almost 30,000 soldiers engaged. By the time fighting subsided on March 9, Confederate forces had been soundly defeated at the cost of some 4,600 immediate casualties and many more later through desertion.

The defeat of General Van Dorn's army cemented Union control of Missouri and northern Arkansas for the next two years. Price's army had suffered many killed, wounded and captured. Defeated and discouraged, thousands of Price's men had had enough of war, deserting and returning to Missouri. With Missouri now in the iron grip of the Union, many of these men, some with their families, headed to the western territories just as gold was being discovered in what became Montana Territory.

Thus, it is likely that the long-standing legend that "the Left Wing of Price's army" came to Montana Territory dates to this Confederate defeat at Elkhorn Tavern and its aftermath. It is ironic that Price's army was, in reality, "the Left Wing of Van Dorn's army." More Missourians would head west as the Civil War progressed, and another surge occurred after the defeat of General Price during his invasion of Missouri in 1864. The term "left wing of Price's army" was used by the first newspaper of Montana, the Unionist *Montana Post*, as well as Republican politicians, and it is clear that a large portion of Price's disintegrating army moved west after the defeat at Elkhorn Tavern, although not as an organized unit. Thus, there is a strong element of truth that men from Price's army swarmed into Alder Gulch and remained until after the war, when the placer mines played out several years later.

After the Battle of Elkhorn Tavern, the remnants of the Fifth Division were ordered forward to join other Confederate units moving to attack Union troops at Shiloh, Tennessee. The Fifth Division arrived too late to participate in the ensuing April 6–7 Battle of Pittsburg Landing (or Shiloh).

Shortly after, Colonels Tom Thoroughman and Alex Davis were commissioned by Missouri's exiled secessionist governor Claiborne Jackson to return to northwestern Missouri to raise more troops for Confederate service to rebuild Price's battered army. On the night of April 14–15, both men were captured by the Federals at the Missouri River while crossing near Jefferson City. The *Fulton Telegraph* reported: "The capture of four important officers returning from the Missouri State Guard included three former state lawmakers attempting to cross the Missouri River to stir up trouble." The "four included Colonel Alexander Davis and Lt. Col. Thomas Thurman [*sic*] of the Fifth Division."

Union brigadier general James Totten provided the official report of the capture of Davis and Thoroughman:

> *Headquarters District of Central Missouri, Jefferson City, Mo., May 17, 1862*
> *Capt. S.M. Preston, Assistant Adjutant-General, Saint Louis, Mo.*
>
> *Captain: I have the honor to report…that about 11 o'clock on the night of the 15th instant a detachment sent out by me for that purpose made prisoners Lieut. Col. Thomas Thurman [sic], paymaster of the 5th Division Missouri State Guard, and Lieut. Col. Alexander Davis, judge-advocate of the 5th Division Missouri State Guard, both of the staff of General Steen, as also a young man who was about to ferry them across the Missouri River. These rebels are suspicioned [sic] (and so strongly that it amounts almost or quite to positive proof) of being emissaries for the purpose of stirring up rebellion in the State of Missouri. Also that every portion of the State will be visited by similar agents of the rebel army and increased vigilance will doubtless be necessary to secure these dangerous*

men. Colonel Davis and Colonel Thurman were both formerly residents of
Saint Joseph, Mo., the former member of the Legislature for two sessions
and the latter circuit attorney of Saint Joseph district. Quite a number
of prominent citizens of this vicinity are implicated in this matter, and
inasmuch as they are prisoners of war (if indeed they are not spies really)
and as it is necessary for them to be kept safely and where they cannot have
communication with their friends implicated in their scheme I recommend
Alton as a very good place where they may be kept.

Very respectfully, your obedient servant,
JAS. TOTTEN, Brigadier-General

After his capture, Colonel Thoroughman was confined in prisons in
Missouri until being transferred to Quincy Prison, Illinois. Strong appeals
were made to President Lincoln for Thoroughman's release, and on
December 13, 1862, the president directed Union officials at Quincy to use
their discretion. The president wrote:

To [Secretary of War] *Edwin M. Stanton*
December 13, 1862

Will the Secretary of War please direct that Mr. Thoroughman may be
disposed of at the discretion of Abraham Jonas and Henry Asbury of
Quincy, Ill., both of whom I know to be loyal and sensible men?

A. LINCOLN
December 13, 1862

Abraham Jonas, of Quincy, Illinois, a brilliant orator, lawyer and friend
of President Lincoln, had three sons who fought for the Confederacy and
one for the Union. Henry Asbury was a law partner of Jonas and also a close
friend of Lincoln, who later named him as Quincy District provost marshal.
The two men had arranged the Lincoln-Douglas Debate of 1858 at Quincy.
At the president's request, Jonas and Asbury arranged Tom Thoroughman's
parole, banishing him to the western territories.

Meanwhile, Alex Davis had been imprisoned in St. Louis for six months before
being pardoned by Governor Willard Hall and moving to booming Virginia City.

During his trip west in the fall of 1863, Thoroughman found his brother
Charles in Denver and then joined brother Oliver H.P. Thoroughman, also a

Confederate soldier, the following spring in Montana Territory. By early 1864, Tom Thoroughman and Alex Davis had reunited in Virginia City, where they operated a law partnership, among the first lawyers in the new territory.

Both Thoroughman and Davis immediately engaged in Democratic Party politics, becoming leaders in the territory's dominant party. In February 1866, Tom Thoroughman was elected to Montana's first constitutional convention. According to the *Montana Post*, this convention, a hopeful precursor to statehood for the fledgling territory, was called by Acting Governor Thomas Francis Meagher to pave the way for Meagher and Thoroughman to be named senators of a new state of Montana. In Washington, D.C., the Republican Congress was not about to admit a new Democratic state in the midst of the war, and Montana would have to wait another twenty-three years to achieve statehood.

With sharply increasing settlement in Montana during the mid-1860s, incidents with the Blackfeet on the Benton–Helena Road and the Sioux and Cheyenne on the Bozeman Trail escalated dramatically. On April 9, 1867, Acting Governor Meagher sought troops from Major William Clinton, who commanded the First Battalion, 13th Infantry, posted the previous year to construct Camp Cooke at the mouth of the Judith River. When Clinton refused to send troops to Bozeman, his letter was read with disgust at a war meeting held on April 18 in Virginia City. Colonel Thomas Thoroughman seized the moment and "mounting a chair, [he] called on all who were willing to accompany him to give in their names at once. In five minutes he had a full company."

Soon several companies were raised and two small posts organized: Camp Elizabeth Meagher (named for the acting governor's wife), located eight miles southeast of Bozeman, and Camp Ida Thoroughman (named for Thomas's daughter), positioned four miles east of today's Livingston at the mouth of Shields River at the Yellowstone River.

Governor Meagher commissioned Thoroughman a brigadier general in the Montana militia in his military orders of April 28, 1867:

> *Thomas Thoroughman on reporting himself to the Undersigned, at Bozeman City, will be appointed to the command of all the troops in the field and on active duty, with the rank of Brigadier-General. He will have the disposition of these troops, and the initiation and control of all movements it may be necessary to undertake—and he…will be respected and obeyed accordingly.*

After Meagher's sudden mysterious death on July 1, Governor Green Clay Smith, in his General Order No. 1 of July 14, demoted Thoroughman to colonel and limited his principal responsibility to the Gallatin Valley to "protect the frontier from Indian invasions." The arrival of the U.S. Army in Montana Territory in 1866–67 relieved the need for a militia—and the fledgling territorial army had fought no battles.

Colonel Thoroughman married his second wife, Miss Mattie L. Boyce, in Virginia City on September 19, 1867, and to this union two sons and three daughters were born. In 1869, Thoroughman returned with his family back to Missouri after his wartime exile years in Montana. The family settled in St. Louis, where he practiced law until his death.

The proud Rebel veteran of the Missouri and Montana militias passed away on December 24, 1896, and rests today in Bellefontaine Cemetery, St. Louis. The Missouri legal community eulogized him as "one of the old Missourians" fast disappearing from the scene:

> *In Col. Thomas Thoroughman's death the bar of Missouri lost one of its most admirable and worthy members…He was of that class fast disappearing from the scene of action, a true and pure American gentleman of the old school…Colonel Thoroughman was one of the old Missourians of this type…you were his friend in ten minutes after you first saw him.*

Chapter 5

FROM A BOYHOOD IN THE CELLARS OF VICKSBURG TO THE MONTANA SUPREME COURT

WILLIAM H. BUCK

By July 4, 1863, the devastating blows of Gettysburg in the East and Vicksburg in the West had sealed the fate of the Confederacy. Although the war would continue for almost two more years, the South had effectively lost.

Both Gettysburg and Vicksburg were battles that affected more than Yankee and Rebel combatants—both directly impacted the residents of the two towns. Fifteen-year-old Will Van Orsdel roamed the battlefield at Gettysburg, dodging gunfire while carrying water to the wounded. Nine-year-old Horace Buck dodged artillery shells and lived underground during the long siege at Vicksburg. Both boys carried the mental scars of warfare for the rest of their lives. This is young Horace Buck's story.

Horace R. Buck was born in Yazoo County, Mississippi, on September 17, 1853, to Charles L. and Maria I. Barnett Buck, both of Huguenot descent. His father, a prominent lawyer, was one of the few members of the Mississippi convention to speak out and vote against the resolution of secession from the United States. The ravages of the Civil War deprived the family of everything and with the death of Charles Buck in 1862 the family struggled to survive. During the forty-seven-day siege of Vicksburg from May 18 to July 4, the family remained in that beleaguered city. With them were thirty-one thousand Confederate soldiers and four thousand civilians, a quarter of them children. Young Horace later related how the shells ranged so close to his family's house that they often were forced to take refuge in a neighbor's cellar for the night. Civilians as well as soldiers suffered from a lack of food and good drinking water.

As Grant closed in on Vicksburg in the spring of 1863, he knew the critical importance of that fortress on the Mississippi. President Lincoln set the tone with the words: "Vicksburg is the key! The war can never be brought to a close until that key is in our pocket…We can take all the northern ports of the Confederacy, and they can defy us from Vicksburg."

In addition, Vicksburg was strategically vital to the Confederacy. President Jefferson Davis proclaimed, "Vicksburg is the nail head that holds the South's two halves together." While held by the Confederacy, it blocked Union navigation down the Mississippi. Together with control of the mouth of the Red River and Port Hudson to the south, Vicksburg allowed communication with the states west of the river, on which the Confederates depended extensively for horses, cattle, other food and reinforcements.

With its natural defenses, Vicksburg earned the name the "Gibraltar of the Confederacy." It was located on a high bluff overlooking a horseshoe-shaped bend in the river, De Soto Peninsula, making it almost impossible to approach by ship. North and east of Vicksburg was the Mississippi or Yazoo Delta, described by geographer Warren E. Grabau as an "astonishingly complex network of intersecting waterways," some navigable by small steamboats.

Since May 18, Grant's army had formed a tightening ring around Vicksburg, sealing it from the outside world. The city was under siege as the noose ever tightened. To hasten Vicksburg's surrender, Grant ordered his artillery to shell it around the clock. With some 220 Union cannon firing at Confederate targets in and around the city, life was dangerous for both the military and civilians, including their slaves. Admiral David Porter's navy joined in with another 13 big guns firing from the river. Militarily, the Vicksburg Campaign was a joint operation, with both the army and the navy playing important roles. The campaign is studied to this day for the bold and innovative joint service tactics that Grant and Porter employed.

Life in besieged Vicksburg was not pleasant. In the words of historian Andrea Warren:

> *Shells flew fast and furious, sometimes crisscrossing in the air as they rained down death and destruction on the city and the Rebel soldiers. Cannonballs weighing as much as 250 pounds crashed through walls, tore up streets and yards, and exploded in the Confederate trenches…Civilian homes could not*

THE REBEL GIBRALTAR.

Fortifications Around Vicksburg, Together with Its Investment by the Union Troops.

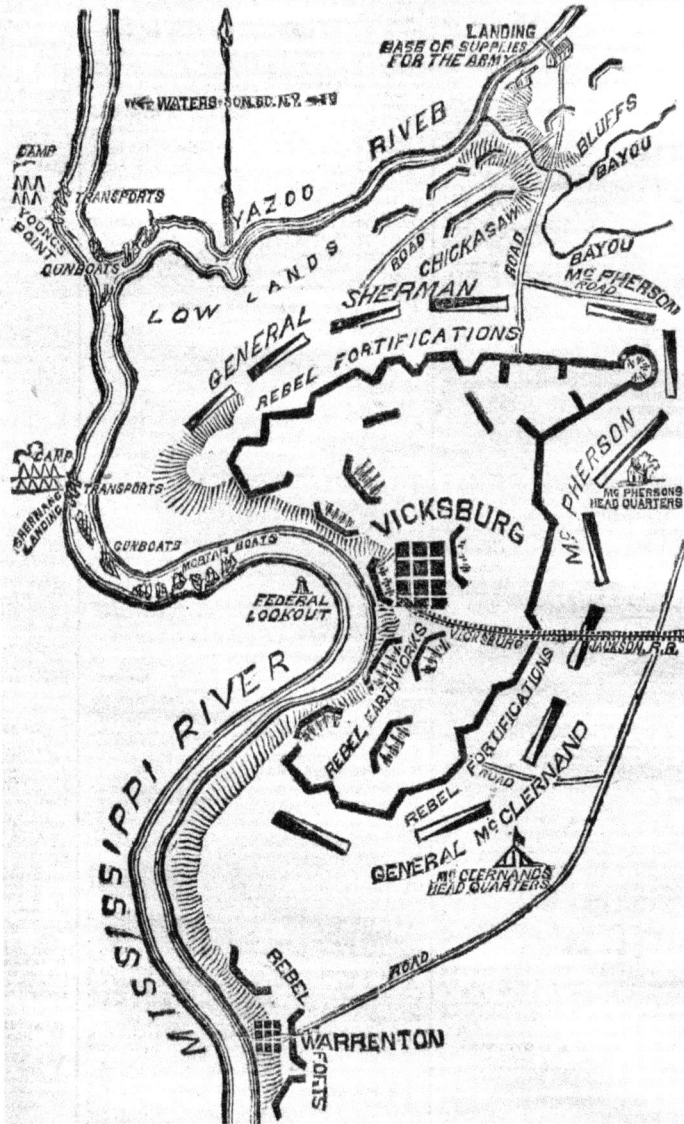

Map of the fortifications surrounding the Rebel Gibraltar, Vicksburg. From the *New York Herald*, June 10, 1863. *Author's collection*.

protect the families. Many families moved into large communal caves that had been dug into the hills.

Other families, like the Bucks, lived in deep cellars. House slaves either slept in family quarters or near cave entrances, as did wounded, recuperating soldiers. Children, like young Horace Buck, played on the dangerous streets or underground while their mothers sought food, sewed and gossiped by candlelight. Slaves tended fires and cooking stoves, preparing meals for their masters, while soldiers brought news to civilians in the trapped, troubled city.

All this time, Mr. and Mrs. Barnett, Horace's grandparents, supported the family, although it was all that they could do. When peace was declared, the Buck family moved to Bayou Teche in St. Mary's Parish, Louisiana. In 1869, the Louisiana plantation had to be sold, and Mrs. Buck took her children to the farm of John Barrett, a relative living near Sedalia, Missouri. While there, Horace attended public schools and then, through the generosity of an uncle, attended Hopkins Grammar School in New Haven, Connecticut, in preparation for Yale University. Graduating from the grammar school in the class of 1872, he entered Yale's class of 1876.

At Yale University, Horace Buck flourished, and in the words of classmate and lifelong friend William R. Hunt, Horace had "great breadth of mind, mature judgment and conspicuously quick perception…No member of his class was more beloved." After graduation in 1876, his uncle was no longer able to assist him financially, so he moved on to St. Louis, where he taught night school to earn a living. He also studied law at St. Louis Law School and in the office of John W. Noble of St. Louis, a brevet general in the Union army. General Noble regarded young Buck as "the best student he had ever known."

Admitted to the bar of Missouri in 1878, Buck joined Hunt in Dakota Territory the following year in search of a place to settle. Being out of money, he found employment as a harvest hand on a large wheat farm. He earned the usual harvest hand's wages but found work on a threshing crew very hard. In the fall of 1879, he became principal of the public school in Shakopee, Minnesota, and remained there until just before Christmas, when he started for Fort Benton with just seven dollars in his pocket. Joining Hunt, the two friends established the law firm of Buck & Hunt.

Buck immediately showed his talent and ambition, taking part in both political and legal affairs. During 1881–82, Buck edited the *Benton Record*, a staunchly Democratic newspaper, and married Mary Jewett, of New Haven.

Horace R. Buck rose from his boyhood in the cellars of Vicksburg to the Montana Supreme Court. *Montana Historical Society 952-567.*

Buck, as managing editor of the *Record*, had Hunt as his associate editor, and as the *Anaconda Standard* later recalled:

> *The "boys" made the* Record *"howl" during the boom days of Benton…Buck devoted his talents in those days to grinding out long and dignified editorials, on intricate financial and social problems of a national character, while Mr. Hunt roamed the streets…startled the good people of the town by* [uncovering local stories]*…and other sensational facts*

of a like nature that always interested patrons of the largest newspaper
published in the territory—a nine-column folio.

In November 1884, Buck was elected to the Fourteenth Territorial
Legislative Council, defeating popular pioneer Robert Vaughn. He became
one of the leading members in the council. Buck was elected Fort Benton
city attorney in 1885, and he led the effort to draft the town's first charter
and organize city government.

While Buck & Hunt built a successful practice in Fort Benton, the limits of
the old river port town were too restrictive for the ambitious young lawyers,
so they moved their firm to Helena in 1887. There, they joined former
territorial governor Benjamin P. Carpenter, forming Carpenter, Buck &
Hunt. Buck also recorded decisions of the Montana Supreme Court, while
Hunt was named district judge. Four years later, Governor Joseph K. Toole
appointed Buck as judge for the First Judicial District in Lewis and Clark
County. For the next decade, Buck served as district court judge until he was
elected to the Montana Supreme Court in 1896, joining Hunt on Montana's
highest court.

On December 6, 1901, newspaper headlines in Helena read, "Judge
Buck Is Dead! Last Night He Sent a Bullet Crashing Through His Brain."
A hastily assembled coroner's jury heard testimony and reported a verdict:
"He came to his death by his own hand, namely by shooting himself in the
head with a 38-caliber revolver, but whether the same was accidental or
intentional we have no means of knowing."

In a tribute to his friend, W.H. Hunt wrote:

> *The inexpressibly sad death of Justice Buck, occurring as it did when*
> *he seemed in ordinary health and vigorous mind, bids us to remember*
> *"what shadow we pursue." In his death the state has lost one whose*
> *pleasing presence was long familiar to those who have had to do with*
> *lawyers and courts, for he was in active practice and judicial service*
> *since 1879.*

The long and close friendship between Judges Hunt and Buck was
remarkable considering the fact that the one had been a Northerner and the
other a Southerner, one a Republican and the other a Democrat. Having
spent their school years together, they went on to become law partners and
were associated as district judges for many years and again as associate
justices of the Supreme Court.

A tribute to Horace Buck came from a committee of six of Montana's leading lawyers: "To the discharge of the duties of this office (associate justice) he brought legal learning, broad general culture, judicial experience and unswerving impartiality."

Judge Buck was a conspicuous figure in the jurisprudence of the state. The boy from the cellars at Vicksburg was no more, yet he left a lasting legacy in Montana. Today, Horace R. Buck rests in Forestvale Cemetery in Helena.

Chapter 6

FROM RIDING WITH COLONEL NATHAN BEDFORD FORREST TO THE NEZ PERCE WAR

PRIVATE JOHN C. LILLY

John C. Lilly fought like a tiger for the Confederacy. He served in the Kentucky Cavalry with Colonel Nathan Bedford Forrest, the "Wizard of the Saddle," in a unit known as Forrest's Old Regiment and lived to tell about it. Addicted to action, Lilly came to the wild Upper Missouri frontier shortly after the war and was never far from danger.

Born John Carl Lillie in January 1844 in Hannover, Niedersachsen, Prussia (now Germany), he immigrated to America in 1858 and settled into farm life in Shelby County, north-central Kentucky. When the Civil War began, Lilly joined with local boys to fight for the South.

John C. Lilly left an account of his service with the Confederacy, and portions of his personal experiences are provided in his own words in this article. Yet Lilly's account is larger than his own experience, as he writes the story of the exploits of his remarkable commander, Colonel Nathan Bedford Forrest. Forrest was a fierce and innovative leader, a brilliant cavalry officer who rose from private to lieutenant general in the Confederate army. He was a superb tactician, a ferocious fighter and a dynamic leader—he killed thirty opponents by his own hand, had twenty-nine horses shot from under him and was wounded on four occasions.

Recruited by Colonel Forrest to join the Boone Rangers, later known as the 1st Kentucky Cavalry (Confederate), a part of Forrest's Old Regiment, Private John C. Lilly rode beside Forrest for most of the war, sharing the thrill of victory, the agony of defeat and the ever-present danger. The stories of Colonel Forrest, Private Lilly and Forrest's Old Regiment are testimony to

After riding by the side of Colonel Nathan Bedford Forrest during the Civil War, Private John C. Lilly came to Montana Territory. *Overholser Historical Research Center.*

the ferocity of the Civil War in the West, which took the lives of many good, brave men from both North and South.

Lilly's diary provides a detailed glimpse of the daily life and activities of a Confederate cavalryman in Forrest's famed Old Regiment. It is a useful reminder that not all immigrant Germans fought for the North. John Lilly began his account:

In 1861 I was living in Shelby County Ky. about three miles from the town of Shelbyville on Clear Creek working for Mr. Henry Harris on a Farm. I was then a boy of about 16 years old. It was then when the whole country was making preparation for war. Kentucky was divided. Some were for the South and some for the North. Especially in the neighborhood where I was then [there was] *a great…sympathy with the South.* [Editor's comments are in brackets. Lilly's creative spelling and punctuation have been "normalized."]

Young Lilly's employer, planter Henry Harris, was staunchly pro-Confederate, listed as owning fourteen slaves—six adults and eight children—in the 1860 U.S. Slave Census. Lilly and Harris's son Gamaliel began drilling with neighborhood boys, preparing to fight for the South. Lilly wrote:

We commenced to drilling as Soldiers and I never shall forget what a good time we had on the Bright moonlit nights, especially in old Kentucky where the moon shines bright up on the old Kentucky Shore. We boys were happy and gay. We had then a different idea of the war than what it turned out to be after we got in to it.

We were progressing fine in our drilling until some time the latter part of June [1861] *when N.B.* [Nathan Bedford] *Forrest came to Louisville and was making preparation and arrangement to organize a Regiment of Kentucky Cavalry…He appropriated a lot of saddles, pistols and some guns. In the meantime while Col. Forrest recruited in Louisville,* [Union] *General* [Lovell H.] *Rousseau was camping and recruiting across the Ohio River, and of course he was posted and informed of every thing that was going on in Kentucky, especially in the surrounding county of Louisville. Col. Forrest had no time to organize his Regiment of Kentucky Cavalry but gathered up what few men there were in readiness to go, and as he had heard of our little party drilling in Shelby County he sent us word to meet him at the Molin Bridge in Hardin Co, Ky., where he then had a little over a hundred men in Camp. I forget the date when we left Clear Creek, but it was in the night. We moved thru Shelbyville but we had to be very careful as the town or the people in Shelbyville were strong Union men.*

Colonel Forrest's colorful call to arms in June 1861 read, "I wish none but those who desire to be actively engaged. COME ON BOYS, IF YOU

WANT A HEAP OF FUN AND TO KILL SOME YANKEES." Avoiding known Union men, the Shelbyville recruits proceeded on their way, stopping only at homes of Confederate sympathizers, where they sought food and fodder for their horses. On the road, the recruits stopped to talk with slaves going to work. Lilly continued:

> There came along some nigros [sic] to go to work on the farm. One of our boys spoke up, "Say Sam," to one of the nigros, "is there any Rebels in this country?" "Well young master," he says, "I don't knows [who] you might be." At that you must remember where every masters were, the nigros were also generally speaking. So Sam told us that his master was for the South and told us of all the people in the neighborhood which were for the South and which were for the North. So we were well posted in that vicinity.
>
> Sam's master was a Mr. Stone, the first house we would come to, and I must say right here that Mr. Stone was Southern from the Crown of his head to the Sole of his feet. Here our horses were fed and a special breakfast gotten for us. I often think about that breakfast, how we devoured that meal. We were never better treated in our life as we were by Mr. Stone and his family. They were happy to see a lot of Boys go to the Southern Army. Anything we wanted, there was nothing too good for us. I had a poor saddle, which was hurting my horse's back. Well, Mr. Stone gave me his saddle almost new, and he took mine in place. While we were eating and resting, Mr. Stone gave us all the instruction where to stop on our whole route and told [us where] we would catch up with N.B. Forrest.
>
> Of course we did the most of our travel in the night. We stayed put one more night at a Farm House on a very good large plantation…It was after 10 o'clock when we rode up, all of us close to the house, and said, "hello" when the gentleman came on the porch. "Is there any chance for us to get supper" was the question. The gentleman did not know what to make of us for it was hard to tell who we might be…but by a little inquiry and telling him whom it was that told us where to stop for our supper. He said, "Boys it is alright. Get down." In the meantime, he called up a half dozen nigros to take care of our horses…In a short time we were called to supper, which was as fine a meal as any one wants to set down to. Our intention was to go on right after supper, but after supper there was nothing to do but what we must come in the parlor and hear the girls sing and play on the piano and of course that was delightful for us boys. We forgot all about the war…we

were insured [sic] by our Landlord that there was no danger of us being trapped or attacked in the night. He made us stop all night, and I believe that himself and a few of his trustworthy slaves stood guard the balance of the night. Anyway, we were not disturbed and had a good night's rest in a fine room and a fine bed.

After breakfast, and a good one at that, we were again invited in the parlor and had more music and songs. Of course they were all Southern songs. When our horses were brought to the porch by the nigros, there were "Three Cheers for Dixie" and the young ladies started "The Girl I Left Behind Me," and then we once more started on the road to Molin Bridge for Camp Forrest.

When we arrived we rode into Camp some time about 10 or 11 o'clock [p.m.]. We were halted for the first time by the pickets, but as the pickets were aware that we were coming there was no trouble for us to go right into camp. That was our first night in a Soldiers Camp. There were about one hundred & fifty men in Camp. Some were sleeping, some were eating and some were setting by the fire smoking. N.B. Forrest was there among the boys laughing and talking. He made us acquainted with some of the boys. We fed our horses, and then we tried to broil, putting it on a stick and holding it over the fire. Everything was plenty, ham & bacon and good strong coffee. There was not much sleep that night…The next morning we were given a new saddle and a Colt's Revolver with ammunition, and then, we for the first time since we left Shelby County, were prepared to defend ourselves from our enemies.

The Shelbyville boys left their horses and boarded trains, passing through Bowling Green, Kentucky, where General Albert Sidney Johnston was organizing the Confederate army. They then rode on to Memphis, camping at the Memphis Race Track and commencing drilling in earnest. Lilly continued:

In about two weeks our horses arrived in Memphis. We were moved to a nice grove about three or four miles from Memphis and commenced drilling on horseback that suited us to perfection. Then we were sworn in to the Confederate Service for 12 months and our Company was Co. A of Forrest Regiment of Cavalry and called ourselves the Boone Rangers. Our officers [were] Capt. Overton, 1st Lieut., John Crother, 2nd Lieut. [and] Wm Wade, 3rd. N.B. Forrest was Col. of the Regiment. Our Company was about 120 men strong. The next company was from

Tennessee, Company B, Capt. May [and] *Lieutenants Jess & Wm Forrest, brothers of Col. Forrest. The next was a Texas Company commanded by Captain Gughle.*

The steamboat *Hill* transferred Lilly's Company A to Columbus, Kentucky, in September 1861. Lilly wrote:

We had a very nice trip with the exception that the boat ran in to a snag somewhere near Island No. 10, which made quite an excitement among the boys thinking that the boat would sink. It happened in the night, and the boat struck so hard that it rolled some of the boys out of their beds. But it was found that there was no danger of sinking and we landed at Columbus.

The next day we were then about three miles from Columbus on the Mobile & Ohio Rail Road. Columbus was well fortified. We thought no boat could ever pass them big guns. I have here forgotten the date when the battle across the Mississippi in Missouri was fought. We were ordered to report to Head Quarters at Columbus to be ready for action. Then we got the first smell of powder from the Big Guns, but we were not brought in to action. At night we were ordered back to our Camp, and then we made our first Scout towards Paducah, Ky. where we for the first time saw a live Yankee. Two Yankee soldiers that were captured by Jeff Thompson's… Rangers… Thompson's Rangers had already accomplished what we were sent for, and we returned to Camp. Soon after that we were ordered to Fort Donaldson on the Cumberland River, where we were doing nothing but drilling every day.

All this time we have not seen our Col. and the balance of our Regiment. Sometime in November we were ordered to Hopkinsville, Ky. where we went into Camp for the winter, and Colonel Forrest organized the Regiment which were two Kentucky companies, one Tennessee, one Texas, three Alabama companies, with Major Kelly of Huntsville Alabama as our Major of the Regiment. We having a good time had good living, fast horses, little camp duty, little scouting thru the surrounding country, and drilling on horseback. That was the best time I have had thru my four years of soldiering, and every one of the boys will agree with me that was camping at Hopkinsville. The People of Kentucky, at that time, would do anything for a Confederate soldier, especially the Ladies…there was nothing too good for a Confederate soldier.

The "Wizard of the Saddle," Colonel Nathan Bedford Forrest. *Library of Congress.*

After this lull in the action, Private Lilly resumed his narrative:

> *But now the tug of war commences. Col. Forrest received news that there were some Union men on the Ohio River making trouble for the Southern men. You must remember that the people of Kentucky were very near evenly divided in their sentiment and also that Kentuckyans were hard fighters. So Col. Forrest concluded to make a raid in to that part of the country. He took*

a detail with himself as leader, marched on thru Princeton, Ky. to the Ohio River into Muhlenberg.

Coming at the head of our column was Col. Forrest and Dr. Cowen, our Surgeon [the regimental surgeon was Dr. Van Wyck, not Cowen], *a young man of Charleston, S.C. A better man could not be found, I don't think, than Dr. Cowen. Our command was halted in a lane when Col. Forrest and Dr. Cowen rode up to the house and called "hello." When the answer was given from within, it was with a Kentucky Rifle, and it struck the doctor right between the eyes. He fell dead from his horse, and before we could surround the house the man came thru the back window and disappeared in the thick timber of the bottom of the Ohio River and never was caught up with. I have forgotten the man's name. The Doctor was the first dead man of Forrest's Old Regiment.*

We camped on that place that night, and of course anything that was portable we took. Some of the boys was ready to set fire to the place, but the Col. would not have it. The next morning we took a wagon and the Doctor was put in to it, and we marched back towards Hopkinsville.

We had gone three or four miles on a different road going thru a lane [with] *Col. Forrest at the head of the column. Coming to a double log house, three shots from old Kentucky Rifles rung out . . . right into the head of our column. One bullet went thru one* [of] *the horse's neck and one thru the arm of one of the boys. The other missed and went close to Col. Forrest's head, but the three fool-hearty men that made such a foolish attack on a column of a hundred men and not stayed in the house and kept up the fire. I should not call* [them] *brave . . . they were foolish, for as soon as they had fired they broke and ran thru timber pasture.*

The rear of our column never thought of laying down the fence, for we had good old Kentucky horses, and they were able to jump any fence. Before the Father and his two sons . . . were a hundred yards from the house, they were riddled with bullets and dead men and left where they fell. Such was the case and times of Old Kentucky in the beginning of the war. After that work, which lasted only five minutes, it was forward march. We camped at Princeton that night and got back to our winter quarters with a record of killing three Unionists and our dead surgeon, one man wounded and a horse shot thru [the] *neck.*

All the men in camp felt very sorry for Doctor Cowen, our young surgeon. He was liked by everyone, officers and privates. So Doctor Cowen was the first man killed of Forrest's Old Regiment . . . there was a different feeling in the men over dead men shot in the beginning of the war than there was later on in the war.

Private John C. Lilly spent Christmas 1861 in Colonel Nathan Bedford Forrest's winter camp at Hopkinsville in relative comfort. However, the reconnaissance, light skirmishes and limited action of the regiment as it protected the Confederate base and capital at Bowing Green would soon change dramatically. Lilly's account continued:

After a few days in Camp the news came to Forrest that the 1ˢᵗ Kentucky Cavalry (Union) were south of Green River in the neighborhood of Greenville under the command of Major More. Col. Forrest, always ready for a fight, ordered three days rations and to be ready to move early the next morning. This time [Colonel Forrest] took, for the first time, his whole Regiment with the exception of a few [men] to do Camp duty and what was on the sick list.

The next morning we started on the road to Greenville…we got [there] and camped at a big hay ranch or farm. It was bad weather in [late] December, with a cold drizzling rain all day and night. A scouting party was sent out that night. They came back and reported the Yankees were close and Captain [Charles E.] Meriwether with an independent squad was "working them" as we called [it] now in the west.

Forrest ordered to sound the bugle for Boots and Saddle. In 10 minutes we were on the road towards Sacramento, Ky. When we got to a crossroad [one mile south of the town], an old farmer and his daughter who were coming from Sacramento told Forrest that the Yankees were but five miles ahead of us. Forrest…sent his orderly back to the other Captains of Co. B and Co. C to come up in good order a little behind our Co. [A]. Forrest then gave the command to our Company by fours double quick march and him in the lead on a fine thoroughbred Sorrel, and he went charging down a lane into our first battle…I was on a Chesnut mare as fine a little Kentucky animal as ever was under the saddle. She was a present to me from Olivia Harris, the daughter of Henry Harris of Shelby County, Ky. This little mare got it in her head that no other horse should beat her, and there were but a very few that could do it. So the little mare struck [out] and passed my company and passed the Col. right straight for Yankee Cavalry.

Right at the end of the lane was a big stand of timber land. When I [was] very near to the end of the lane, the Col. saw that I was going right into the Yankees. He called to me to pull her into the fence corner, which I did just in time. When the Sorrel came to a halt near the rear guard of the Federal Cavalry, Col. Forrest jumped off his horse while I tried to get my mare quiet. He says, "Give me your gun," which I handed over. He fired into the enemy, gave back my gun, and was mounting at the same time.

The Yankees fired at the same time, but the balls went over our heads… [As] *we dashed forward into the edge of the timber, to our surprise they were formed in a splendid line of battle. Before we could form a line, they gave us a volley and kept it up.* [This] *being our first engagement to face the enemy in such close quarters, they had the advantage on us in position with the exception that the ground* [was] *so situated that they fired too high. Under this fire we tried to form in line,* [but it] *was almost impossible. Col. Forrest and our Lieutenant Ward had their horses shot. Being afoot,* [they ordered] *us not to run. If the Yankees had made a charge that moment, they would have demoralized us right there.*

Captain Meriwether had got to the front with a few men, and one of his men [Private W.H. Terry] *and himself were killed and two wounded were laying in the road. By this time Captain May of Company B had formed in our right when they drew our fire. So we got in line, and fighting was pretty severe for five minutes when Captain Gughle with Company C came up the lane in good order by fours. When Forrest ran back and got Capt. Meriwether's horse,* [he] *says to Capt. Gughle, "Capt., charge them!" When Capt. Gughle gave the command to his Texas Rangers, "Charge them boys," they then gave the Rebel yell, which went thru the woods echoing* [so loud] *that you could scarcely hear the sound of the rifles. When the sound of that yell from the Texas Rangers reached the ears of the Yankee Cavalry, that was too much for them, and our battle was won. That splendid line of battle in Blue was broken and retreating in bad order thru the little town of Sacramento, Ky.*

Right here in the streets of this little town there was a hand-to-hand duel with sabers which perhaps is not on record or in the history as the Yankees…but those were Kentucky Yankees and as brave of men as ever faced a gun or used a pistol or drove a saber which was shown.

Right in that little engagement at the outskirts of this little Kentucky town met Col. Forrest in the lead of his command, victorious, and Captain Backer in the rear of his command, defeated. With sabers drawn, they both went at it, as foes would meet. As Captain Backer was better fighting with a sword, as Forrest found out in a few minutes or seconds, I might say I think that and believe Col. Forrest would have ready left that field of life. But in such conflict where it is in such close quarters it was a pistol ball that ended that saber duel between Col. Forrest and Captain Backer, when the brave Capt. tumbled off his horse a dead man. The supposition is that the shot that killed Capt. Backer was fired from a man of our Company, his name I will not mention.

Here the battle was ended in a glorious victory for Forrest and his Old Regiment. I have forgotten now the number of prisoners we took. I think that the Yankees lost in that fight between forty or fifty killed, wounded, and prisoners. Our lost, I believe, was three killed and five wounded and a few horses killed…Imagine here that there never was a prouder Regiment in the Confederate Army than Forrest's Old Regiment of Cavalry, and the old Col. himself, after that fight, thought that he could lick the whole Yankee army.

That same day, we marched back with our prisoners to Greenville. The next day we started back for Hopkinsville to our winter's quarters, going through that little town called Cloverport [Kentucky on the Ohio River] *which I shall never forget, though I have never been or seen it since. The ladies of that place gave us the finest picnic in the winter that I have ever been to before or since. I never saw as much fine eatables in my life, and we were supplied with socks, mittens, gloves, blankets—most everything forced on to you, whether you wanted it or not. God Bless the people of Cloverport, Ky. is my wish today. In fact, in the beginning of the war the people of the South could never do too much for a Confederate soldier, and especially the women.*

When we got back to our winter quarters, the first news was that there was a gunboat going up the Cumberland River. General [Charles] *Clark had some Infantry camping at the Hopkinsville Fairgrounds with a few pieces of artillery…Col. Forrest wanted to capture that gunboat with his Cavalry. His idea was to capture that boat and then go down the river under the U.S. flag and destroy the whole Yankee fleet at Paducah, Ky. and at Cairo, Illinois, which I believe he would have done if we could have got away with the Yankee gunboat.*

Private Lilly provided a detailed account of this bizarre attempt by Forrest's cavalry to capture a Yankee steamboat. Although ultimately their trap did not succeed, it did result in the death of a dozen of the steamboat's crewmen and damage to the gunboat. Lilly concluded this story, noting "one of our cannon shots had bored a hole thru the boat. So that ended the charge of Cavalry charging a gunboat on the Cumberland River where we [did] not lose a man."

Lilly's narrative continued:

We landed again with triumph in our camp. The people of the surrounding country and of Hopkinsville would visit our Camp and thought that Col. Forrest and his Cavalry were the heroes of the Southern Confederacy. Then we had a good time in camp, [with] plenty of good rations and fat and slick horses [and only] a little camp duties and drilling to do. [We] got passes to go out in the Country and see the girls, who thought more of Forrest's Cavalry than they would of themselves. Who would not be a soldier under such circumstances…but as God knows we saw some hard times afterwards.

Subsequent events would have a profound impact on the outcome of the Civil War. Two legends emerged from the action in Tennessee in early 1862. The North would finally find a "fighting" general in Ulysses S. Grant, while the South would find a legend in the daring and determination of Colonel Nathan Bedford Forrest. The Union devised a critical strategy to seize control of the river highways of commerce in the western theater, including the Ohio, Mississippi and Missouri Rivers. This campaign began with a major operation to seize control of Fort Henry on the Tennessee River. A major linchpin in Confederate general Albert Sidney Johnston's defense lines, Fort Henry was attacked by Union naval gunboats and surrendered after most of its guns were disabled. While most Confederate troops were trapped at Fort Donelson, mainly because of indecisiveness by Rebel commanders, several thousand Rebels did escape, including Forrest's Old Regiment through decisive action on the part of Colonel Forrest. The loss of Forts Henry and Donelson was a stunning defeat for the Confederacy, opening western and middle Tennessee as well as most of Kentucky. General Grant had seized the initiative, forced the Confederates out of Kentucky, broken their defense line in northern Tennessee and permanently changed the strategic situation in the West. And the men of Forrest's Old Regiment were knee-deep in the action. Private Lilly continued his narrative:

From now on our hard times begin. Five days of the month of February [1862] have passed, and rumor in camp is that [Brigadier General] Grant is marching on to Fort Henry. Another day and orders were given to cook up three days rations. The next day we were marching to Fort Donaldson over the same road that we came over five months before to go into our winter quarters. Before we crossed the old Cumberland River, we

This Union gunboat fired the first shot at Fort Henry and participated in battle at Fort Donelson. *From* The Photographic History of the Civil War, *Vol. I.*

could hear the cannon booming at Fort Henry fourteen miles distant. We were taken across on a steamboat the next morning, one company at a time. When our Company got across, Col. Forrest started immediately out on the Fort Henry road. About six miles out, we met the Yankees and fighting commenced. We skirmished all day and fell back at night when our whole Regiment was across the River.

We camped that night in a kind of a ravine but worked all night building breastworks for the Infantry. All the next morning, the Yankees advanced [so] that the Infantry got to skirmish with them. Then the gunboats came up and attacked our batteries on the River, and the Infantry [attacked] by land. But the Yankee Fleet got the worst of it, and five of their boats were sunk and others disabled so that they were poled off. The gunboats made it pretty warm for us but with very little harm to us. We were not there to charge gunboats.

The battle for Fort Donelson had begun. Private Lilly's story continued:

Then the next morning, we were completely surrounded by Grant's army, and fighting commenced in earnest with Forrest's Cavalry on the extreme left. By noon, the enemy were driving [us] from the field. About noon, a Regiment of [our] Infantry took a battery from the 7th Iowa. As it happened then, the Confederate Regiment gave out of ammunition and could not hold the Battery. As the Battery was right at the head of a deep ravine and as the 7th Iowa was in the Ravine and was about to retake the guns, Col. Forrest led one of the grandest Cavalry charges on the 7th Iowa Infantry. The charge was made by placing two companies…to charge up to that ravine and fire, one company to wheel to the right, and the other to the left in the ravine…and load while the other platoon would charge right here.

That brave Capt. May of Company B fell before the charge was made and several of our brave boys beside him. The 7th Iowa gave us a terrible fire while we were forming in line, and it stood time in hand for the move what was coming if they could keep us from forming in line. Reinforcement was coming for them, and they would have retaken their battery, but Forrest with actually tears in his eyes led the charge, and the 7th Iowa was very nearly all slaughtered in that famous Death Hollow.

When the roll was called of the 7th Iowa after that charge of Forrest's Cavalry into that Hollow of Death, there were not many to answer to their names, and so it was the same with Forrest's Cavalry. If [you have] never been in a battle, you have no idea what it is to form a regiment of Cavalry—especially under heavy fire, especially in timber and brush as it was at that battleground. But we were victorious for a short time.

As the Yankees retreated, we marched down that same ravine, and [I] must say that it was almost impossible for our horses not to step on a dead man. It was but [a] short ravine, yet it was horrible to look at the brave men in the different shapes and positions where they were laying.

As we were following up the retreating Army, which was but a short distance, General Grant massed a heavy battery on a hay hill and turned loose on us all at once before we knew what was going on. We were wheeled right about by fours to get out of range of that heavy artillery fire. Shells and solid shot was whistling over our heads—ranging a little too high but close enough that the boys would dodge—when Col. Forrest made the remark, "Don't dodge, Boys." When he had hardly said the word, a shell came so close to his head that he could not help from dodging. Then he looked around with a smile and said, "Boys, dodge them if you can," which the boys never forgot all thru the war.

We were then marched back inside our camp and thought that Grant was retreating. Firing had ceased with the exception on our left near the river bottom, where General Buckner with his Infantry was doing some hard fighting, and the Motor Boats would throw a few shells into our camp when the night closed the battle. If you have read the history of the battle of Fort Donaldson, you must know that the object of attacking the Yankees' right wing and going out of our breast works was to open the road to Nashville and for our Army to retire. Such was the plan of Generals Pillow, Floyd & Buckner, and Col. Forrest to cover the retreat of the Infantry, but that was not carried out and was without a doubt a mistake of General Pillow's, as he was Commander in Chief.

That Saturday night [the fifteenth], everything was quiet, but it snowed about three or four inches about twelve o'clock at night. No bugle was sounded, but every man was called from under his blanket of snow to be quiet and get ready to march. The generals had agreed for Genl Buckner to surrender the troops, but Col. Forrest had no notion to surrender. In one hour from the time that we were notified, we were in line when Forrest spoke, "Boys, the Confederate Forces have surrendered and the white flag is now floating over Fort Donaldson. After our hard fighting yesterday and the brave men that we left on the field, I have concluded not to surrender. We may have a hard time to get out, but any of you that want to follow me, Forward March."

And the Col. moved on, but I don't think that there was over five hundred of the Old Regiment that followed. Some were killed. Some wounded. Some had their horses killed or wounded. Col. Forrest followed close up the River without any trouble until we came to a large slough, which was full from the backwater of the old Cumberland River and partly frozen. We were fired into by a Michigan Regiment of Cavalry, but they could not stop Forrest and his men. Forrest and the advance guard [rode] right into the backwaters, and the balance followed. Some had [to] swim their horses, and some could even ford them. The charge on the Michigan Cavalry took them by surprise as it was not daylight yet, and in a short time we were behind the Yankee Army. I am not able to tell whether we lost any of our men or not, as we did not know who followed in our retreat. And as far as the Yankee Cavalry, we did not lose any time to get out after we got thru the Yankee lines. We could hear the bugles and the drums in our ears. So far Col. Forrest had escaped from Fort Donaldson, but what was before him he did not know.

That part south of the Cumberland River is a broken country ridged by hills and deep ravines. [It was] not much of a farming country, [but] there were five old Iron Furnaces. Forrest could not get much information when we got near Charlotte, [but] the report was that there was a Yankee Regiment of Iowa Cavalry. Forrest knew that we were not very well fixed for giving battle. We were all wet from crossing the slue, our guns and ammunition were wet, and everyone was worn out, having not slept any for four nights. Col. Forrest halted and had us fire our guns and pistols and clean them for action.

When that was done, it was "Forward March." In the meantime, we did not enter the town [of Charlotte] and struck out for Clarksville. Before we got near Clarksville, we found a lot of baggage and camp outfits that was left by [Confederate colonel John S.] Scott's Louisiana Cavalry [1ˢᵗ Louisiana Cavalry Regiment] that had been ordered to Fort Donaldson. Finding out that it was surrendered, [Scott's cavalry made] a kind of a hasty retreat. Forrest found out that Clarksville was floating the white flag, and as we could see black smoke on the River, he concluded to go on to Nashville. We had quite a time to get the horses fed and feed for ourselves, so we marched night and day when we got in sight of Nashville.

The report came to Forrest that Nashville was in the hands of the Yankees. There were no Yankee gunboats there, but Forrest was [uncertain whether] it was full of Yankee Cavalry. I shall never forget the remark of that daring Col. Forrest just before he got to the bridge of the Cumberland River. He formed his little broken up Regiment in line. There were also a few Infantrymen that had followed us on foot. Poor fellows, what a hard time they had. After he had all of us in line, he says, "I am going in to that town. I don't care if there is ten thousand Yankees in there, and any of you that don't want to follow me fall out of ranks right here. Forward march." I don't know of anyone falling out.

We marched into Nashville [on February 18] without any trouble or fight [the town was not in Union hands]. Col. Forrest made arrangements for us to camp at the Penitentiary, and rations were cooked for us in good style, but it was not necessary for us to eat there. Forrest's Cavalry was welcome at any family table in the town [because] there was nothing too good for Forrest's Cavalry. We were the Heroes of the day. But here it seemed to some of the boys that the war was over, and it would have been a good thing if it had been. I found out afterward that it had hardly commenced, and by this [I] believe that the war [really] was over. As we were the favorites of the citizens of Tennessee, our Regiment, or what was left of it, got somewhat scattered having a good time among the good people of Tennessee.

We got back together at Murfreesboro, Tennessee, camped there for a short time, and then marched to Huntsville, Alabama [arriving February

The Battle of Shiloh, fought in April 1862, was the bloodiest engagement of the Civil War at that time. *Library of Congress.*

25]. *There we were reorganized and the Old Regiment got some recruits. All the scattered boys caught up, and the Old Regiment once more looked natural. From Huntsville we marched to Burnsville, Mississippi. Here we camped without tents, as we had lost everything we had at Fort Donaldson. It was raining day and night, and we did not know what was before us. We had no idea that Grant and his Army that we left at Fort Donaldson was in [but] a day's march of us, and that he was camping at that Old Shiloh Meeting House. But Col. Forrest was always ready if there was any fighting to be done.*

We got to the battleground [at Shiloh] Saturday night [April 5], and there met a rain, but it cleared up nice and bright. Col. Forrest's Cavalry was detached to [Major] General John C. Breckenridge's Command. Sunday morning was a most beautiful morning after all the raining for five days before had made everything green. At daylight a few shots were exchanged, and before we knew it was volley after volley. In a short time, Col. Forrest at the head of his Regiment double quicked to Hamburg on the Tennessee River to guard the rear of Breckenridge to prevent the Yankees from landing troops. In the rain we had no trouble with the exception of the gunboats shelling us, and through all of it Forrest was primed. He could tell by the firing that our men were driving the Yankee Army before them, and he wanted to be in it.

We were thrown out as pickets all along the ridge and the river. It was not long when we were called in, and Forrest at the head of his column marched double quick for the battlefield. He got there just in time again to make a grand charge. This was made by Col. Forrest leading the charge across an old field over which there had been a great contest, but it was won then. Col. Forrest lost two horses that day.

Brigadier General Benjamin M. Prentiss had saved Grant's army that first day at Shiloh. Prentiss's division dug into a sunken road at the center of the "Hornet's Nest" and held off the Confederates for six critical hours. Forrest was in on the capture of Prentiss and two thousand of his men, but the Confederate advance had been delayed at the Hornet's Nest. Lilly continued:

When Genl. Prentiss surrendered, firing had slacked off to almost as if everyone had left the field. Everything was quiet when all at once General Breckenridge moved his whole line forward on towards Pittsburg Landing, and Col. Forrest with his Old Regiment in line [formed] behind Breckenridge. When this column of Infantry and Artillery and Cavalry marched forward in line of battle, it was a grand sight to look at.

It seemed that nothing could stand in front of that victorious line of men, but as that was the last stand of Grant's defeated Army that day, they made a noble stand. They waited until our lines got in short range and the grandest sight of all was that the sun was about setting, and it looked red when a person looked right into it. Then at once the guns of the Yankees belched out fire, shot, and shells that were terrific. Our Infantry fell to the ground and our Batteries opened [up]. That was one of the grandest artillery duels by the setting of the sun that most every one will ever see.

As the Yankee artillery fire stopped the forward movement of our Infantry, they turned their fire on Forrest and his Cavalry that was rather a little too much for the Cavalry to stand. Where Infantry can lay down, Forrest would not move, [so] horses and men were shot down till Genl. Breckenridge ordered him to fall back out of the range of the Artillery of the enemy's guns. Col. Forrest fell back a distance out of range when the Artillery duel was going until well after dark. Then after dark, Forrest moved in front of our Infantry and Artillery right close up to the Yankee guns. Here we were standing out as a chain picket for the night.

Everything was quiet, but have you ever been on a battlefield? If you have not, you can not imagine the feeling that every one will have that stands within two hundred yards of an enemy. Now and then you hear the sound of a wounded man crying for water or calling on God or cursing and swearing, and then you hear some owl that has escaped the fire of the day.

The night after the first day's fighting at Shiloh was a terrible night after the sun was down and everything was dark. Big black clouds began to race in the west, and it was not long when it began to rain and thunder, and lightning was terrific. The Yankee gunboats kept up a cannonading from their big guns, throwing shells in every direction with but a little harm to us. It sounded and looked more dangerous than it was. Here we were within two hundred yards of the Yankee lines and shells [exploding] all around us, and thunder and lightning and heavy rain came down on us. It made a man feel kind of funny, but as we thought that all of our Infantry and Artillery was right close behind us, where we left them after when we marched in front of them, it kept us in good spirits.

Confederate forces were so sure of victory at the end of that first day of fighting at Shiloh that Confederate commander General P.G.T. Beauregard sent a telegram to President Jefferson Davis announcing "A COMPLETE VICTORY." Meanwhile, General Grant's nerves of steel were reflected in a story told by Brigadier General William T. Sherman. At the end of that first day, Sherman found Grant under a tree, sheltering himself from the heavy rain. Grant was smoking one of his cigars while reflecting on his heavy losses and planning tactics for the next day. Sherman remarked, "Well, Grant, we've had the devil's own day, haven't we?" Grant glanced up. "Yes," he replied, puffing on his cigar. "Yes. Lick 'em tomorrow, though." Private Lilly continued his account:

When daylight came, we found ourselves very much mistaken. When we began to look around, there was not a man in sight. Our whole Army had fallen back. How far we did not know. Our picket closed up and were formed in line of battle. Col. Forrest ordered us to fire off our guns, as they were all wet. Before we got thru with these, the Yankees were advancing in double quick time. They threw out a half skirmish line, and the balance of the Yankees marched in a column while we gave them the best we had but would never stop them from coming right for us.

Forrest would fall back a short distance and form in line and wait for them to come close enough. Then [he] *would give them a volley and fall back again a hundred yards and do the same thing over till at last, to our surprise when we fell in line, we were right in front of our Infantry skirmish line. This surprised the Yankees, who commenced to form in line of battle. Forrest and his men were holding them in check when the Yankees were putting a Battery in position and opened up on us when Forrest fell back.*

This time we fell back of our Infantry lines, where we went into camp long enough to feed our horses and ourselves, dry ourselves as much as we could, and clean our guns. But before we got off our horses in camp, the battle was raging where we had left. The Infantry and Artillery got together in good shape.

During the evening of the first day's fighting, General Don Carlos Buell's fifteen-thousand-man army arrived and was shuttled across the Tennessee River by steamboat to Pittsburg Landing. Colonel Forrest tried during the night to warn his commanders that Union forces were being greatly reinforced, but his warnings were ignored. Monday morning, April 7, began, and Private Lilly reported the turn of the tide of battle in favor of General Grant's Union forces. Private Lilly summarized the disastrous second day:

That was Monday [April 7], *the second day of Shiloh,* [which] *was the hardest day of fighting as ever was done on any battlefield in history. It was hard for the Confederates to give up the ground that was won the day before, but the Yankees were determined to take back what they had lost.*

With 25,000 fresh [Union] *troops* [Buell's fifteen thousand and earlier arriving soldiers from Major General Lew Wallace's division], *they were partly successful as the Confederates were slowly driven back. When before night came* [on that second day], *the Battle of Shiloh had ended. Forrest was always in the thickest of the fight. Monday night, Forrest and his Regiment were rested, but at daylight Tuesday morning, Forrest and his men were in front of the Yankees again* [in a battle called Fallen Timbers, April 8, 1862]. *In a charge that morning, Col. Forrest was badly wounded, but he rode to the rear. His horse was killed also.* [Forrest took a rifle ball in his left side just above the hipbone. It lodged on the left side of his back near the spine.]

Col. Forrest was taken to Memphis, but his old Regiment stayed on the field doing picket duty. Every now and [then], *we made a little dash on the Yankee picket, and they would do the same on us. As it would happen, the Yankee Cavalry in front of us on picket [duty] was the 1ˢᵗ Kentucky that we had defeated at Sacramento, Ky. Our Captain was sent in with a Flag of Truce by General John C. Breckenridge. He took ten men of his Company [and] I was one of them.*

While our Captain was going to the Yankee Headquarters, we were having a great chat with the boys of the 1ˢᵗ Kentucky. Some of our boys were school mates of some of them. While we were chatting with the boys, waiting for our Captain to return, the boys of the Yankee Cavalry all at once jumped for their horses ready for a fight.

Before we knew what it meant, we saw a separate Confederate Cavalry within a hundred yards of us and the Yankee pickets. But immediately we saw a white flag, and the excitement was all over. These [men] were from the famous John H. Morgan, also with a flag of truce for General Grant's Headquarters. John Morgan had nothing but a squadron of about 150 men.

In the meantime, our Captain got back, and we returned to Breckenridge's Head Quarters which was then at Pinnock, Miss., only five miles from the Shiloh battlefield. We were doing picket duty here for a long time, Major [David C.] Kelly being in command of our Regiment. From here we fell back to Corinth, Miss. When one day we were surprised [to see] Col. Forrest arrive in Camp. Although he was looking a little pale, we were glad to see him back to take command of the Old Regiment. Col. Forrest was considered somewhat ruff with his men, but there never was a better officer to provide for his men. In camp or on a march, we always had plenty of grub and horse feed. He would make the Quartermaster hustle.

While General [Henry W.] Halleck was advancing slowly on to Corinth from the Shiloh battlefield, Beauregard was sending his troops to reinforce General [Robert E.] Lee in Virginia. When Halleck got to Corinth, there was nothing there but Forrest with his Regiment of Cavalry. General Sterling Price had moved out to Farmington on the Mobile and Ohio Rail Road. Price offered battle to General [John] Pope. We had quite a set too, but General Price fell back to Tupelo, Miss. When Forrest with his men had quite a hard fight at Guntown, the Yankees fell back to Corinth, and we camped at Tupelo.

The Battle of Guntown (or Brice's Crossroads) pitted Forrest's 4,800-man contingent against 8,100 Union soldiers under Brigadier General Samuel D. Sturgis. Though outnumbered, Forrest used better tactics to defeat the larger

Private Lilly's Forrest's Old Cavalry did some hard fighting at the Battle of Corinth in October 1862. *Library of Congress.*

Union force, delaying the invasion of Alabama and Mississippi by Union forces. Private Lilly continued his narrative:

> *Here we were reorganized and sworn in for twelve months or* [the duration of] *the war. Myself and a lot of our Company were under age, but we stuck to it. Two of our boys went out on that account but substituted and were transferred back to our Company.* [In the Confederacy, substitutes at times could be paid to serve in the army.] *Our Col.* [David C. Kelley] *left us, detached to General Price's Command, and* [Colonel] *Forrest went with* [General Braxton] *Bragg to Kentucky. We were then again under General* [Earl] *Van Dorn, and when Price and Van Dorn fought the battle of Iuka* [September 19, 1862] *and also the* [Second] *battle of Corinth* [October 3–4], *our Regiment done some hard fighting.*
>
> *We were also on that grand move of Van Dorn's on to Holly Springs* [December 20, 1862], *which was one of the grandest moves made during the war. We then belonged* [to] *General Frank Armstrong's Brigade. That winter we done duty in Mississippi. In the spring* [of 1863] *we were*

marching back in to Middle Tennessee when we met our old Col. Forrest, but now he was a General and a good one, commanding two Brigades.

Our first fight we got in to here was at Thompson's Station, not far from Franklin, Tennessee. Here we were again victorious and captured a whole Brigade of Infantry [under Colonel John Coburn]. Right here we camped in the garden spot of Middle Tennessee. General Van Dorn [was] in command of all the Cavalry [with] Head Quarters at Spring Hill, but as misfortune would have it General Van Dorn was shot and killed by Dr. [James Bodie] Peters [on May 7, 1863, for carrying on an affair with Peters's wife]. General Van Dorn was the best cavalry commander in either Army. He would have proven it if he had lived.

From here, we fell back to Tullahoma…of course we were skirmishing and fighting all the time. From here, we crossed the Cumberland Mountain and got to Chattanooga, where we were camping and scouting in to East Tennessee until the Battle of Chickamauga [September 19–20, 1863]. Here Forrest formed his Cavalry on our right, dismounted, and we fought as Infantry. A Yankee Battery in front of us was making us lots of trouble, but dust of the roads and the powder smoke of that battle was so thick that it was impossible to see over twenty feet ahead of you. But it seemed that the Battery had it in for us all day. Of course our line was so thin that there was not much fighting, but some heavy skirmishing. Late in the evening, Forrest concluded to teach that Battery, and he took the lead and we charged the Battery. The Yankee retreated to the rear but left two pieces of cannon.

As we were not able to hold our ground, we were falling back to our first position. But that Battery did not fire any more on us, and later before dark, we were relieved by General [Lieutenant General James] Longstreet, who was very much surprised to find Cavalry in line of battle as Infantry. That night we were moved a little further on the right of Longstreet's Corps. The next morning, [Major General William S.] Rosecrans had left not a Yankee in sight. General Forrest was right after them, but they had too much head start, and the main Yankee Army was already in the town of Chattanooga. We captured a good many stragglers until all at once we were in to an ambushed Infantry and Battery, which opened up on us with grape and canister.

General Forrest dismounted part of his men and charged the rear guard of Rosecrans, but while our men were charging on foot, the Yankees retreated. Forrest with the mounted men charged after them. By that time, the Yankee Cavalry faced Forrest. In the meantime, the balance of our Cavalry that was dismounted came up and the Yankee Cavalry retreated. General Forrest *with five men charged right into the edge of the town and brought out a lot of Yankee prisoners with some officers. Right there General Forrest wanted permission to charge the town, but General Bragg would not let him. Still he made another dash from under the point of the Lookout Mountains. The Yankees opened up with a Battery that they had captured in Tennessee, which was too much for us.*

After this, we were marched into East Tennessee, where Gen. Forrest found Gen. [Ambrose E.] *Burnside's Army that was marching from Knoxville threatening Gen. Bragg's rear. General Forrest was doing some hard fighting to hold Burnside in check. In the meantime, the Battle of Lookout Mountain and Missionary Ridge was fought and lost by Gen. Bragg and put Gen. Forrest in between the Armies so that he had to make his way out. But there was no rest in Forrest. He swung around into North Alabama, crossed the Tennessee River and made a raid thru Middle Tennessee, where he was making lots of trouble for Grant's Army, got a few recruits and some fresh horses, and destroyed the Rail Roads and supplies of the enginemen. We came back very near over the same route that we went, crossed the Tennessee River at the same place above Florence, Alabama and moved into winter quarters to rest our horses near Rome, Georgia.*

It was but a short time when Gen. Sherman moved on to Tunnel Hill and Dalton, Georgia. When Forrest took position in Sherman's Front and fought in front of Sherman all spring until the Battle of Atlanta on July the 22ⁿᵈ 1864. [At that time, Union Major] *Gen.* [George] *Stoneman, Jr. was getting in the rear of Gen.* [John Bell] *Hood and intended to get to Macon, Georgia to destroy the Confederate Arsenal at that place.*

John Lilly's diary ends at this point, though he likely was in on the Stoneman operation. General Stoneman was captured while on a raid outside Macon, Georgia, attempting to free Union prisoners of war at infamous Andersonville Prison. Stoneman became the highest-ranking Union officer captured during the Civil War.

Lilly's diary concluded by lauding his hero, Nathan Bedford Forrest: "There never was a man in that war as a General that done any more daring deeds and hard fighting then General N.B. Forrest of the Confederate Army. By John C. Lilly Co A—Forrest's Old Regiment."

Private Lilly fought on to the end of the Civil War and the defeat of the Confederacy. Lilly joined the exodus westward, coming up the Missouri River to Fort Benton in the late 1860s. By 1870, he was working on a farm in the Sun River Valley.

Frontiersman John Lilly was addicted to action. *Author's collection.*

At the end of the 1860s, Fort Benton had a dozen saloons and one brewery in operation. A decline in mining in Montana Territory resulted in less demand for goods and supplies, and this hit the Fort Benton economy hard so that by the mid-1870s, there were only four saloons. Despite this decline, Fort Benton remained a wild and wooly place, especially during the spring and summer steamboating season. John Lilly operated one of the popular saloons, dispensing cards and whiskey in conjunction with a dance hall. The other saloons included J.C. Bourassa and Phil Deschamps's The Exchange; L.T. Marshall's The Elite, where, in 1872, with four well-directed bullets, Marshall killed Dennis Hinchey, "a notorious character of the border" who "wouldn't be missed," as a coroner's jury ruled by acclamation. The fourth joint was the Extradition Saloon of John Evans and Jeff Devereux, famed for its celebration of the release of whiskey traders from Canadian custody.

Several years later, in 1877, Lilly operated Brinkman & Lilly's Billiard Saloon, which featured "the finest of wines, liquors, and segars." While Fort Benton was beginning to evolve into a tamer town than it had been, it was still one rough place.

During the summer of 1877, the Nez Perce War involved both the military and civilians in Fort Benton. That summer had seen a tremendous upswing in steamboat traffic on the Missouri, and the resurgent activity brought a building boom to Fort Benton. Residents had followed closely the saga of the Nez Perce as they moved eastward through Montana Territory. Bentonites took keen personal interest when elements of the 7th Infantry Regiment, including mounted infantry under First Lieutenant James H. Bradley, departed Fort Benton and Fort Shaw to engage the Nez Perce in western Montana. All residents of Fort Benton knew and liked young Lieutenant Bradley, who had been stationed at Fort Benton Military Post. News of Lieutenant Bradley's tragic death on August 9 at the bloody Battle of the Big Hole brought the war home to the town in a very real way.

As the Nez Perce moved rapidly northward through the Judith Basin toward the Missouri River on their flight to the Canadian border, they encountered elements from Companies B and F of the 7th Infantry Regiment, a mounted civilian volunteer company led by the Fort Benton Military Post commander and Civil War veteran Major Guido Ilges, and freighters on the Cow Island Trail. Overall, these men constituted a small, dispersed force, and historians have largely ignored their actions. Yet their encounters at Cow Island and Cow Creek Canyon, coupled with the decision by the Nez Perce to slow their pace of advance, enabled pursuing U.S. Army cavalry and mounted infantry to catch and capture most of the Nez Perce at the Bear's Paw Mountains.

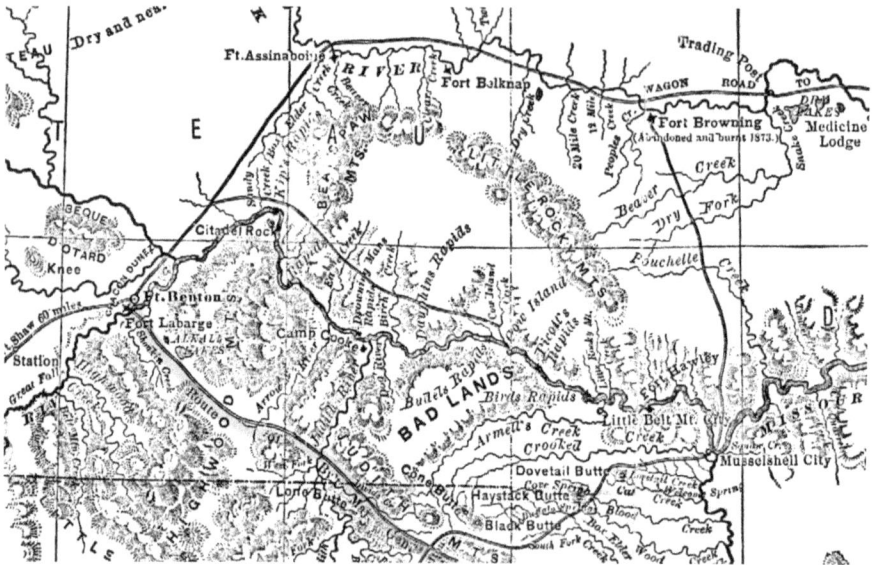

Map of the Upper Missouri River region. *Overholser Historical Research Center.*

Cow Island, an important cargo discharge landing during low-water season on the Missouri River. *Overholser Historical Research Center.*

Early on the morning of Friday, September 21, interpreter Cyprien Matt rode into Fort Benton with news from James Wells of Fort Claggett that the Nez Perce were traveling up the Judith Basin headed for Canada. Wells asked for help to protect the fort, a trading post at the mouth of the Judith forty miles above Cow Island and eighty-six miles below Fort Benton. Major Ilges, with a depleted Company F, directed Lieutenant Edward E. Hardin with thirteen men, plus two volunteer boatmen, to load a twelve-pound mountain howitzer onto a mackinaw boat and set off downriver to Fort Claggett.

Major Ilges, with Private Thomas Bundy of Company F, and twenty-four citizen volunteers, known as Donnelly's Company of Mounted Civilian Volunteers for their fiery Irish Fenian leader and Civil War veteran John J. Donnelly, departed Fort Benton on horseback at 7:00 o'clock Friday evening. The Ilges force traveled twenty-four miles to the springs beyond the Marias River, where they encamped at one o'clock in the morning. The *Benton Record* newspaper reported the movements and warned, "It is hardly possible that a handful of men sent to protect Fort Claggett and Cow Island can give them [the Nez Perce] a very serious check."

Former Confederate cavalry private John C. Lilly and other ex-soldiers joined Donnelly's Company looking for a fight. Major Ilges and Donnelly's Company broke camp at daylight on Saturday, September 22; rode all day; and arrived at Fort Claggett at 5:30 p.m. after covering fifty-six miles. On Sunday, September 23, the Ilges, Donnelly and Hardin forces remained at Claggett, awaiting the return of their scouts. Toward evening, the command was strengthened by the arrival of six more volunteers from Fort Benton.

At two o'clock on Monday morning (September 24), the scouts finally returned to report that the Nez Perce were moving toward Cow Island. Ilges's command left at daylight and traveled all day downriver, reaching the banks of the Missouri opposite Cow Island by evening. Soon after going into camp, Lieutenant Hardin's force arrived by mackinaw, bringing the mountain howitzer.

At daylight on Tuesday, September 25, the Ilges and Donnelly force crossed the Missouri by mackinaw to the north bank. At the landing, they found that the Nez Perce had burned Cow Island depot and strewn supplies over the surrounding hills. The nearby rifle pits showed signs of a fierce struggle. Major Ilges dispatched a courier to Colonel Nelson Miles and started on the trail leading up Cow Creek. His objective was not to intercept the overwhelming Nez Perce main force but to locate and protect the slow-moving ox-trains and a light wagon with steamboat passengers.

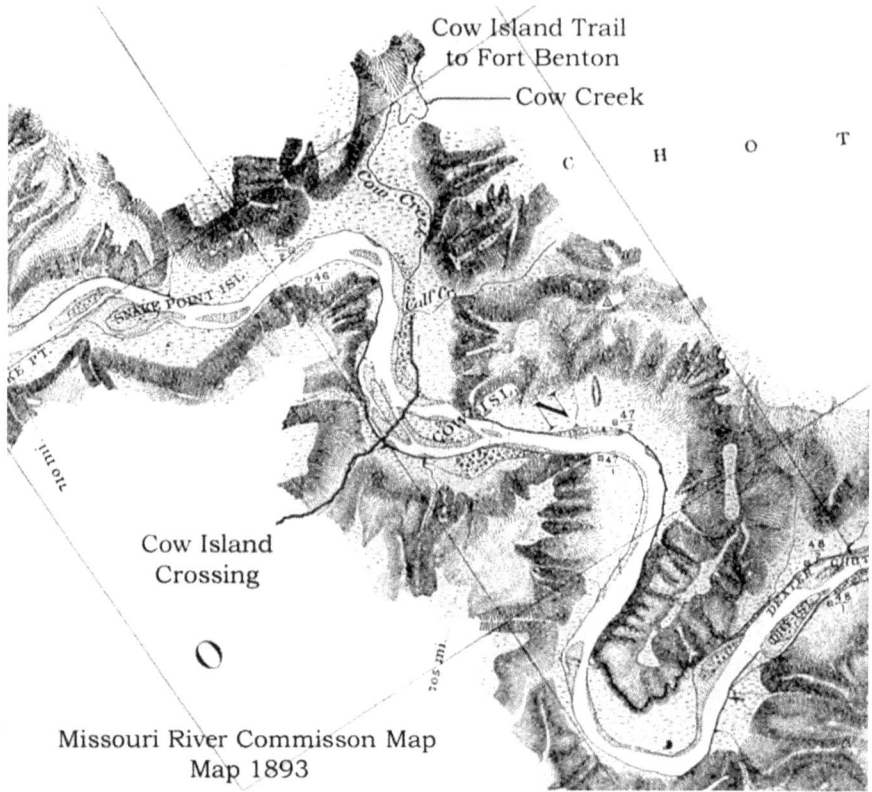

Map showing the route of the Nez Perce crossing of the Missouri River at Cow Island. *Overholser Historical Research Center.*

While Ilges's men were en route to Cow Island, the Nez Perce broke camp, moved up Cow Creek and, by noon on Monday, had overtaken the Farmer & Cooper wagon train, slowed by a muddy trail, numerous crossings and a herd of cattle. The Nez Perce went into camp near the train ten miles up Cow Creek.

Early Tuesday morning, Major Ilges moved with Donnelly's Company up Cow Creek, leaving Lieutenant Hardin, twenty-five men and the howitzer at Cow Island. Scout Murray Nicholson spotted the Nez Perce camp, and as the Ilges command approached, the Nez Perce took action against this perceived threat to their camp. Warriors shot and killed teamster Fred Barker, while seven other teamsters retreated into willow cover. The warriors ransacked the train and set fire to the wagons. Major Ilges halted his command as he observed the Nez Perce camp readying to depart. By noon, the Cow Creek Canyon fight was underway. As the main Nez Perce camp moved away, warriors began firing on the Ilges command from the bluffs above. Ilges deployed his force into defensive positions. For over two hours, firing continued. A Nez Perce sharpshooter killed black American Edmund Bradley. John Tattan, another volunteer, came close to death when he was knocked down by a bullet strike to his abdomen, stopped by his belt plate.

As soon as Major Ilges decided to stand and fight, he sent Private Bundy back with orders for Lieutenant Hardin to bring up his men and the howitzer. Bundy safely covered the dangerous ten miles in less than two hours. After firing in the canyon ceased about 2:00 p.m., the Nez Perce warriors moved north, while Major Ilges withdrew down Cow Creek to meet Lieutenant Hardin's detachment. The small combined force continued back to the Cow Island rifle pits to defend further Nez Perce attacks and to guard newly arriving steamboat freight while awaiting the arrival of Colonel Miles.

On Wednesday, September 26, most of the volunteers returned to the Cow Creek Canyon battlefield to bury Edmund Bradley and Fred Barker. The remainder worked to strengthen and enlarge the rifle pits at Cow Island. In the evening, the steamer *Benton* arrived and commenced discharging sixty tons of freight.

At noon on Thursday, Major Ilges with Donnelly's Company departed Cow Island to return to Fort Benton. They passed the burned wagon train and found the wagons and their contents entirely destroyed. The Ilges command made a night march, reaching Bear's Paw Springs about 11:00 p.m. After the volunteers left the canyon, the Nez Perce rear guard attacked Hilda A. Nottingham's train, which was en route to Cow Island from Fort Benton. Nottingham managed to escape and turned the train back toward Benton.

On Friday, September 28, the Ilges command marched until midnight, reaching Twenty-four Mile Springs. Early Saturday afternoon, about 1:00 p.m., Major Ilges and Donnelly's Mounted Company with John Lilly reached Fort Benton. They were "tired, worn, but cheerful, and ready to start again if their services are needed." The *Benton Record* was full of glowing praise:

> [Our] *Bold Volunteers…fully deserve the gratitude of this community and the General Government. They have not annihilated Joseph and his band, but they have accomplished a great deal of good. They relieved Fort Claggett* [and then] *relieved and strengthened the party at Cow Island. They have by their action saved two steamboats and 100 tons of government freight.*

They have fought the Indians on their own ground and harassed them in their movements. They have developed the enemy's position and strength, they have saved the lives of the trainmen by their prompt advance, they have buried the dead, they have demonstrated to the Indians the fact of our strength should mischief be intended in this direction and, by their return, they have gladdened the hearts of our people beyond expression.

In fact, the modest military and civilian force from Fort Benton proved of significant value in distracting and delaying the northward movement of the Nez Perce from the Cow Island area. This, coupled with the decision by the Nez Perce to slow their advance for precious hours after their hectic race northward through the Judith Basin, proved fatal and enabled Colonel Miles's forces to catch and force their surrender at Snake Creek near the Bear's Paw Mountains.

For the rest of the 1870s, John Lilly remained in Fort Benton, and in 1880, the Copperhead Democrat–controlled *Benton Record* described Lilly's new business:

Lilly's Billiard Hall was opened to the public last night. The best music of the town entertained the visitors. An elegant supper was furnished in the rooms in the rear of the hall. Several new bartenders volunteered their services, many of whom added tone to the house, while others were entirely lost amidst the multitude of glasses and bottles. The opening was one of the grandest ever witnessed in Benton. Yogoites [gold miners from Yogo City], *Mongolians, Greasers, Coons, Whoop Uppers* [from Fort Whoop-Up], *Assinaboins, Coal Bankers, book fiends, lawyers, kickers, mule-skinners, bullwhackers, rangers, cow boys, Indian-traders, and butchers were all represented.*

In 1881, Lilly moved and renovated a bar on Main Street formerly kept by Lee Isabell into "a neat and attractive resort." Each evening, a string band played "sweet music" for the patrons of Lilly's Barker District Saloon, named for the recent rich silver strikes at Barker in the Little Belt Mountains.

In January 1882, John Lilly started for Barker, the silver mining camp. For the next year, he spent time in both Barker and Fort Benton before settling down for a long residence in Barker. Lilly opened a brewery to supply the thirsty miners and began ranching. In 1884, he married Miss Katie Henn, and they raised a family of seven children. By 1886, Lilly served as postmaster at Barker, a post he retained until 1906, when the post office was closed. At various times, Lilly also operated a hotel at Barker and served as justice of the peace and notary public. Unlike most residents of the once lively camp that had lost its luster in the Panic of 1893, Lilly and his family continued to live at Barker and operate a ranch several miles from town. Even though the mining camp had closed, the diggings abandoned and the railroad taken out, Mr. and Mrs. J.C. Lilly never lost faith in Barker and were among a handful of residents remaining.

By the winter of 1906–07, Lilly's health was failing. He died in May 1907 at age sixty-three at the Columbus Hospital in Great Falls. The old Confederate veteran Private John C. Lilly from Company A, Colonel Nathan Bedford Forrest's Cavalry Regiment, who left an impressive account of his wartime exploits was interred at Cavalry Cemetery in Great Falls and later reinterred at C.E. Conrad Cemetery in Kalispell, Montana. With the passing of John Lilly, the United Confederate Veterans lost a fierce fighter and Montana a colorful pioneer.

Note: Private Lilly's commander and hero, Colonel Nathan Bedford Forrest, settled in Memphis, Tennessee, after the Civil War. Antebellum slave trader Forrest lost most of his fortune during the war. He found employment with and eventually became president of the Marion and Memphis Railroad. Less successful in business than in combat, Forrest's railroad went bankrupt. By early 1867, Forrest was active in the Ku Klux Klan and may have served as grand wizard of this infamous night-riding, quasi-military white supremacy organization.

Chapter 7

QUANTRILL RAIDER AND TRAIN ROBBER LEFT DEEP TENTACLES IN MONTANA

JAMES BERRY

The border war between Missouri and Kansas, known as Bleeding Kansas, was a series of violent confrontations from 1854 to 1861 involving antislavery "free-staters" or "jayhawkers" based in Kansas Territory versus pro-slavery "border ruffians" or "bushwhackers" from Missouri. Bleeding Kansas was a proxy war between Northerners and Southerners over the issue of slavery. It set the stage with the outbreak of the Civil War for special animosity and violence in both Kansas and Missouri. Jayhawkers raided Missouri farms thought to be pro-secessionist, freeing slaves and wreaking havoc. Bushwhackers raided towns and farms of Kansas, burning and pillaging them. The conflict became one of total unconventional warfare, sweeping though the civilian population with an unmatched ferocity.

Despite the fact that Missouri's governor favored secession and pro-secessionist officers led the state's militia, the state remained in the Union at the outbreak of the Civil War because of decisive action by Union troops stationed in St. Louis. Along the Missouri River corridor, a large slave-owning area known as "Little Dixie" remained in insurrection throughout the early years of the war. For the Confederacy, the Missouri State Guard under General Sterling Price conducted much of the fighting. Supporting the partisan rangers of the state guard were quasi-military units such as William Clarke Quantrill's Raiders and "Bloody Bill" Anderson's men. These units wrote their own rules of warfare and often dressed in civilian clothes or Union uniforms. They left a bloody trail as they employed the hit-and-run tactics of guerrilla warfare, often taking no prisoners.

Brothers Isaac (Ike), Richard (Dick) and James (Jim) Berry grew up in Callaway County, Missouri, in the heart of Little Dixie. James F. Berry was born in 1838 near Shamrock, Callaway County, the fifth of ten children of farmer Caleb and Virginia Fulkerson Berry. By 1860, James was off the farm, owning and operating a grocery store in nearby Williamsburg.

As with many unconventional forces of the Confederacy, few records were kept and even fewer survive concerning Quantrill and Anderson's men. Post–Civil War reconstructions, such as the William Pennington List, offer insight into those who likely served in the war with both Quantrill and Anderson. Among Quantrill's men were soon-to-be famous outlaws Jesse and Frank James and the Younger brothers.

Pennington's List includes the three Berry brothers, together with Samuel Morgan Hays, husband of their sister, Rebecca Berry, with brief notes:

> *Berry, Ike (Isaac). Was at Lawrence* [Kansas] *with Quantrill, Centralia* [Missouri] *with "Bloody Bill" Anderson 9/27/1864. Purportedly convinced Anderson to burn Danville* [Missouri] *10/14/1864. Survived War, becoming a liquor merchant/restaurateur. Died 1928, Missouri.*

> *Berry, Richard. With "Bloody Bill" Anderson Unit. Survived War—was with Quantrill at Lawrence* [Kansas]. *Brother of Ike.*

> *Berry, James. With "Bloody Bill" Anderson Unit. Rode with the Sam Bass gang after the war, robbing banks and trains throughout the mid-west. Killed, Oct 21, 1877, by Sheriff Glasscock in Adrian County, Missouri.*

> *Hays, Samuel Morgan. With Quantrill. Indicted 18 Nov 1863 for the murder of George Burt at Lawrence* [Kansas], *21 Aug 1863. Sam was married to Rebecca Berry.*

In his book *Sam Bass & Gang*, historian Rick Miller writes: "[Jim Berry] was reportedly a member of Bloody Bill Anderson's guerrilla troop, associated with the infamous Quantrill's raiders in Missouri during the Civil War." Years later, in 1877, the *Sedalia Weekly Bazoo* reported:

> *Jim Berry's bearing was that of a man who would fight to the last. Indeed, he had given previous examples of his desperate and daring nature. He was one of Bill Anderson's most daring followers, and his unshrinking courage was tested in many a terrible fray which that bold partisan led all into who followed his banner.*

The *Missouri State Journal* added:

> *Jim Berry was known to have been one of the most desperate members of that terrible company of rough-riders who followed the fortunes of Bill Anderson during the war, and they also knew that he had two or three brothers living in Callaway who were fully as dangerous as he.*

Miller writes also of the close relationship of Bill Anderson and Ike Berry:

> *According to the St. Louis* Daily Missouri Democrat, *12 November 1864…*[Bloody Bill] *Anderson's "orderly" was a man named Ike Berry, whom he called "Weasel." Both Anderson and Berry were intoxicated and together severely pistol-whipped and tortured Lewis, and Anderson even rode a horse over him until the family was able to produce five thousand dollars. Lewis died, largely as a result of his injuries, on February 2, 1866.*

As sketchy as these sources are, it is clear that the three Berry boys served under Quantrill and Anderson during the Civil War, and only the toughest rode with them. It seems clear also that Jim Berry served only briefly in the war before heading to the western territories, while Ike and Dick Berry continued to fight for the Confederacy throughout the war.

By late 1861, William Quantrill had formed a raider force that included the three Berry boys and their brother-in-law Sam Hays. During the winter, his force grew in strength to around two hundred well-mounted and armed men. Throughout 1862, Quantrill and his men raided around Kansas City, Independence and Olathe. After a raid on Independence on March 19, 1862, the Union issued a general order that all guerrillas were to be treated as common criminals rather than soldiers and prisoners of war, and they were to be shot on sight. This "no quarter" policy apparently was a turning point for Quantrill and his men. Until then, they often had paroled prisoners, a common practice by both sides early in the war. After the authorities issued the "no quarter" order, Quantrill and his men exercised the same policy of no quarter toward their captives, usually killing them on the spot.

Hoping to convince the Union to soften its policy toward guerrillas, the Confederate government passed the Partisan Ranger Act. The act legitimized guerrilla bands as rangers acting under the authority of the Confederate army. The Union army command ignored the Partisan Ranger Act, but from that time on, the men who rode with Quantrill and similar bands considered themselves soldiers in the Confederate army, and the CSA bore responsibility for their actions.

In July 1862, the Union issued Order No. 19, requiring all able-bodied men in pro-slavery Jackson County to enlist in Missouri Union militias and help exterminate the guerrillas. This was at a time when marauding Kansas jayhawkers, operating as Federal militia, were preying on slaveholding families in Jackson County. Order No. 19 led many young men in Jackson and surrounding counties to flood into the camps of Quantrill and General Price's Missouri State Guard.

On August 11, 1862, Quantrill led twenty-five veterans and four hundred new recruits into Independence. The Union commander surrendered his force to a Confederate officer present. Four days later, Quantrill was commissioned captain, and his men were mustered into the Confederate army as partisan rangers, part of Colonel Joe Shelby's 2nd Missouri Cavalry Regiment. This unit, to which Jim Berry belonged, was also designated the 12th Regiment, Missouri Cavalry, CSA, informally known as the "Jackson County Cavalry" since most of its men came from Jackson County. Although Colonel Upton Hays—and later Colonels Beal G. Jeans and David Shanks—commanded this cavalry unit, it remained closely associated with Quantrill and his raiders.

Five days later, on August 16 at the Battle of Lone Jack, Missouri, Quantrill's Raiders joined the Confederate army in defeating Union forces. On September 12, Quantrill raided Olathe, Kansas, killing fourteen while sacking and looting the town. The 4th Kansas Cavalry chased the raiders for ten days through four counties in Missouri. Throughout the early fall of 1862, Quantrill's men were chased relentlessly by the 4th Kansas and 6th Missouri Cavalries.

During the summer of 1862, Bill Anderson formed his own gang, robbing to support themselves and killing Union soldiers, and Anderson quickly earned the sobriquet "Bloody Bill." Early in 1863, Anderson traveled to Jackson County, Missouri, to join Quantrill, yet initially Quantrill gave Anderson a chilly reception, as he perceived Anderson to be brash and overconfident.

In May 1863, Anderson's gang joined Quantrill's Raiders on a raid near Council Grove, Kansas, in which they robbed a store west of town. After the robbery, a U.S. marshal with a large posse intercepted the raiders about 150 miles from the Kansas-Missouri border. In the resulting skirmish, several raiders were captured or killed as they split into two groups to return to Missouri.

Quantrill's raid and the destruction of Lawrence, Kansas, August 21, 1863. From *Harper's Weekly*, September 5, 1863. *Author's collection.*

During the early summer of 1863, Anderson was commissioned lieutenant, serving under Quantrill in a unit led by George M. Todd. It is possible that the Berry boys were serving under Anderson by this time, although this is not certain. During June and July, Anderson took part in several raids that killed Union soldiers in Westport, Kansas City and Lafayette County, Missouri.

On August 21, Quantrill led his force of about 400 men into Lawrence, Kansas, the strongest abolitionist city in the state. The attack had been carefully planned with independent columns approaching in a coordinated pre-dawn attack. Over four hours, the raiders pillaged and set fire to the town, killing about 185 civilian men and boys, most of the male population, while burning about a quarter of the city to the ground. Their main target, jayhawker Senator James H. Lane, escaped death by racing through a cornfield in his nightclothes.

By 9:00 a.m., the raiders were on their way out of town. The Lawrence Massacre was one of the bloodiest events in the history of Bleeding Kansas. The city seal of Lawrence commemorates Quantrill's attack with a depiction of a phoenix rising from the ashes of the burnt city. Quantrill led his force along the Texas Road en route to winter quarters in Texas. Along the way, on October 6, they fought a minor battle at Fort Blair in Cherokee County, Kansas.

While Ike and Dick Berry were among the raiders who participated in the infamous raid on Lawrence, Kansas, it is likely that Jim Berry had already left the war behind, traveling west to Nevada. Sometime during mid-1863, Jim Berry arrived in mining camps around Reese River, Lander County, in central Nevada. There, on November 26, 1863, he married Mary Elizabeth Price. Mary had moved by wagon train from Callaway County, Missouri, to Austin, Nevada, in 1861 with her father, Cyrus, and brothers, Kyle and Charles. The Price family had likely known the Berrys in Missouri, and Cyrus Price determined to leave Little Dixie after the suicide death of his wife and before his family became swept up in the war.

Jennie Lee Berry, the first of the couple's six children, was born in the Reese River Valley on August 30, 1864. Shortly afterward, Jim Berry with his family joined the gold rush to Montana Territory. Berry's activities in frontier Montana from 1864 to 1867 are sketchy, although in May 1867, twin daughters Anna Natalle and Adelaide "Addie" Price Berry were born in Virginia City.

During the summer of 1867, Jim Berry returned overland to Missouri. His wife, Mary, and their three children traveled from Virginia City to Fort Benton to board a steamboat to go down the Missouri River to return to their home near Mexico, Audrain County, Missouri. The steamer *Gallatin* departed Fort Benton on September 2 with the Berry family on board. Mrs. Elizabeth Meagher, wife of recently deceased General Thomas Francis Meagher, was also on the steamboat, which carried a total of eleven ladies and six children.

The *Gallatin* departed Fort Benton for Omaha with 150 passengers and upward of a quarter of a million dollars in gold dust on board. Slowed by late season low water, the boat reached a point thirteen miles below Camp Cooke at the mouth of the Judith River on the morning of September 5. Here, the *Gallatin* ran hard on the rocks at Holmes Rapids, and for six days the crew and passengers worked with block, tackle and spars, struggling to get it afloat. On Sunday, September 8, the steamer *Only Chance* came along, and about twenty-five of the *Gallatin*'s passengers opted to take passage down on that boat. It was an action they would later regret.

By Wednesday, the *Gallatin*'s crew and passengers had strained and racked the boat so badly that it was considered unsafe to remain on board any longer. All passengers and freight were put ashore and the boat dismantled,

Mining boomtown Virginia City, the capital of Montana Territory, in 1866. *Library of Congress.*

right down to the deck planking. Later passenger accounts spoke highly of the conduct of Captain Sam Howe, who worked day and night in the cold weather and water to save his boat and secure some semblance of comfort for the passengers.

The female passengers, including Elizabeth Meagher and Mary Berry, along with the children, provisions, baggage and a few male passengers, boarded two mackinaw boats. The balance of the travelers started overland on foot to reach the steamer *Huntsville* at Cow Island, fifty miles below.

Approximately eight miles downriver, the mackinaws met Captain Jacobs of the *Huntsville*, coming up with a yawl to their relief. He agreed to carry passengers to Omaha for seventy-five dollars.

Having no cooking utensils, the mackinaw party, including Mesdames Meagher and Berry, laid down to sleep about eleven o'clock that night, hungrier than was pleasant. Adding to their discomfort, the rain coldly and continuously poured down on them throughout the night, while wolves howled in the distance. Berry family legend tells that Mrs. Meagher shared her buffalo robes with Mrs. Berry to wrap her six-month-old twins in the robes, saving their lives.

The mackinaws reached the *Huntsville* by 10:00 a.m., while the overland travelers, hungry, weary, wet, foot-sore and demoralized, came struggling in by squads until nightfall, thankful for their deliverance from a shipwreck on the Upper Missouri. The *Huntsville* then waited for the arrival of the ship's clerk and additional travelers from Fort Benton.

Boating conditions on the Upper Missouri late in the season were horrible. The steamboat *Imperial* was hard aground twelve miles below Cow Island on September 14, with poor prospects of getting off. Another steamer, the *Zephyr*, was above Cow Island, and many believed it would have to remain in the mountains all winter. The *Only Chance* had a terribly rough trip down to Cow Island, pounding over rocks all the way. It left Cow Island on September 12 and made its way down to Omaha, the passengers (including the twenty-five from the *Gallatin*) suffering all the way from poor-quality food leading to much sickness and two deaths from dysentery. One passenger recorded that "a gladder set of boys never walked a steamboat plank" upon their arrival at Omaha on October 4. On board were over two hundred passengers and about $3 million in gold treasure.

The steamboat *Huntsville*, with Elizabeth Meagher and the Berry family aboard, departed Cow Island on September 19 and passed Fort Peck nine days later. The boat worked its way down the Missouri, slowed by the late season low water, the almost constant need to spar across sand bars and frequent high winds. At long last, the trip from hell ended at Omaha on October 17. The Berry family continued on to Missouri by train after their life-threatening trip down the Missouri River.

The Berry family reunited back in Missouri and remained settled on their rented farm near Mexico. The July 1870 census recorded the Berrys as living on a stock ranch at Bassett's Mill, El Paso County, Colorado Territory. Another child, Nora Dickinson Berry, was born in March 1870, followed by son John R. Berry in December 1871. Both were born in Mexico, Missouri.

Wandering Jim Berry again left his family about 1875 for the Black Hills. For a time, he operated a grocery store with a partner at North Platte, Nebraska. This business suddenly folded after Berry and his partner swindled money from a prominent customer. Jim Berry was on his way to a life of crime.

Berry joined the Black Hills gold rush, yet by the early spring of 1877, he had failed to strike it rich. Earlier that winter, young Sam Bass and his boss, Joel Collins, had arrived at the booming new town of Deadwood, Dakota

Territory, after having driven a cattle herd from Uvalde County, Texas. Collins sold the cattle and paid off his cowboys. Deadwood was a tough, wide-open gold mining town populated by miners, cattlemen, adventurers and gamblers. Collins had bought his cattle on credit from friends in Texas, and he owed most of the money he'd received for them. Yet while drinking, he gambled away the money he'd received for the herd. Bass and Collins decided to stay on in Deadwood, playing poker for a living and enjoying life in the boomtown. Collins built a house and bought a quartz mine. The mine proved a dud, and Collins realized his money was gone. He became desperate and, with Sam Bass, decided to form a gang. They tried mining and failed. They tried freighting and failed. Out of desperation, the fledgling Collins-Bass gang decided to rob stagecoaches.

Known as the Black Hills Bandits, the gang consisted of Joel Collins, Sam Bass, Jim Berry, experienced stagecoach robber Jack Davis, Bill Heffridge, Canadian Tom Nixon, Frank Towle and Reddy McKimie. Historian Rick Miller described Jim Beery as being "5' 9" or 5' 10", 180 pounds, [with] sandy or red hair with a little gray in it, a sandy beard and moustache with a long chin beard. He had a red florid complexion, blue eyes, talked a great deal, and when he was drinking his full, round face became quite red."

The Cheyenne and Black Hills Stage Company ran a stage line to and from Deadwood, making an attractive target for the new gang. Traffic each day brought nine Concord coaches, each carrying some eighteen passengers. The first task for the gang was to steal good saddle horses, and this they were able to do.

After biding their time, the gang decided to strike on the evening of March 25, 1877. Under cover of darkness, they rode two miles out of Deadwood and hid in the brush. Hearing the clatter of the coach approaching, the bandits charged from the brush and challenged the driver to stop. From this point on, their plan fell apart. Reddy McKimie, against orders, shot the coach driver. The horses bolted down the road, leaving the robbers afoot. Two trailing mounted armed guards, alerted by the shot, rode up to the scene as the Collins-Bass gang fled into the brush.

Despite this disastrous beginning, the gang continued to rob coaches all through the summer, with only modest success. After six more robberies, they had little to show for their dangerous efforts. After deciding to move on to train robberies, Jim Berry and Collins rode to Ogallala, Nebraska, so that Berry could acquire a new pair of boots. He entered the store of shopkeeper and part-time detective M.F. Leech and asked for the boots on credit. Leech

Quantrill guerilla and Sam Bass Gang outlaw James Berry. Sketch by David Parchen. *Overholser Historical Research Center.*

refused, and Berry and Collins had to scramble to pay for them. Detective Leech would later play an important role in Berry's story.

On September 18, 1877, Collins conceived, planned and carried out one of the boldest train robberies that had occurred in the United States up to that time. When all was ready, Jim Berry and the rest of the Collins-Bass gang, heavily armed and masked, held up the Union Pacific express train at Big Springs, Nebraska, a small station a few miles beyond Ogallala.

The *Mexico Weekly Ledger* reported the sensational train robbery a month later on October 18 under the headline "One of the Pacific Train Robbers

Captured. Our Sheriff a Terror to the Banditti. Frantic Attempt of Berry to Escape":

> *Omaha, Neb., Sept. 19—News reached* [Omaha] *at an early hour this morning that a Union Pacific express car on the morning train that left Cheyenne yesterday about 2 p.m. was robbed at Big Spring by masked men with drawn revolvers, who threatened to shoot Messenger* [Charles] *Miller, compelled him to unlock the safe containing $60,000 in cold coin, and succeeded in escaping with the whole amount.*
>
> *The telegraph operator at the station was compelled to break his instrument to prevent his reporting the occurrence. A half-dozen men were in the party. They went northward, but it is believed to be a feint, and it is believed that their ultimate destination is southward. E. Moreman* [E.M. Morsman], *superintendent of the Union Pacific express office, offers a $10,000 reward for the capture of the parties and the return of the money.*
>
> *Account From Cheyenne. Cheyenne, W.T., Sept. 19.—Big Springs, the station where the robbery of the express train was committed last night, is a water station 162 miles east of this place. There are only one or two houses besides the station. The robbers rode to the station in the evening, and took possession of everything, tearing the telegraph instruments out and throwing them away. A red light was then hung out to stop the train, which reached there about eleven o'clock. On the conductor's stepping out to see what was wanted, he was confronted by men who ordered him to throw up his hands. The engineer and fireman were secured and a guard placed at the end of the coach door. The station agent was compelled to knock on the express door, and on its being opened for him, the robbers rushed in, overpowering Messenger Miller and taking possession of the car. They secured SIXTY FIVE THOUSAND DOLLARS in coin and about $300 in currency from the express car. The through safe, which is stationary and has a combination lock, they left undisturbed. It contained a very large sum of money.* [In fact, Miller was brutally beaten for not opening the safe.]
>
> *The arrival of a freight train evidently interfered with their plans, for after putting out the fire in the locomotive of the express train they mounted and rode away without disturbing the occupants of the sleeping car.*

After the robbery, the gang split up, with Jim Berry making his way back to his home near Mexico. On arrival, the unshaven, dirty and weary Berry checked into a hotel in Mexico, carrying heavy saddlebags that he would not entrust to a porter. He got a haircut and shave with a goatee and mustache trim. He ordered $300 worth of groceries and arranged for them to be delivered to his family on the farm about twenty miles south of town. Berry also ordered a suit at Blum's store. The day after his arrival in Mexico, just as soon as the town's three banks opened, Berry made a fatal mistake by trading in $9,000 in gold coins for currency. Berry explained his bonanza by claiming that he had struck it rich mining in the Black Hills. The banks shipped the coins to St. Louis, where they were quickly identified as likely having come from the Big Springs robbery. Just three days after trading the gold for currency, Detectives M.L. Leech and others arrived in Mexico to confer with the Audrain County sheriff, Henry Glasscock.

The *Mexico Weekly Ledger* of October 18 continued its account of the pursuit and capture of Jim Berry:

> *Monday, Oct. 15, 3 o'clock, p.m. We have just interviewed* [Sheriff Henry Glasscock] *and J. Berry, concerning the arrest of Berry, Sunday morning* [October 14], *and we give you the facts…*
>
> *It appears that last Saturday night* [October 13] *as our Sheriff was eating supper about half past six o'clock, he received a message that a man was in town after the suit of clothes Berry had left at Blum's. The man's name was Bose Kazy* [or R.T. Kasey], *and he lived near Berry's. He told Blum that Berry had told him that he could have the clothes if he would pay the balance of $30 due on them. This was the way he had his "job" fixed up. Glasscock ran right down to Kabrick's Hall and hid behind the counter and saw Kazy come out,* [at] *half past seven. Glasscock followed him to Wallace & McKenny's livery stable. Just as Glasscock got near the stable, he met John Carter and told him to come along. Carter, Glasscock and Kazy all got to the stable at the same time. Kazy paid for his horse feed and started to get on his horse. Sheriff Glasscock took Kazy by the collar, presented a pistol to his head and told him he would shoot him if he moved. Kazy did not move. Glasscock ordered two more horses saddled. They then tied Kazy on his horse and the cavalcade moved off, Glasscock leading Kazy's horse.*

Sheriff Glasscock recruited three more men for his posse. Kazy insisted he knew no more of Berry's plans but stated that he would take the sheriff to Kazy's home. The fact that Sheriff Glasscock felt he needed to raise a posse brought comment about Berry in the *Sedalia Weekly Bazoo* of October 23:

[Berry's] *bearing was that of a man who would fight to the last. Indeed, he had given previous examples of his desperate and daring nature. He was one of Bill Anderson's most daring followers, and his unshrinking courage was tested in many a terrible fray which that bold partisan led all into who followed his banner. Indeed, so great was the terror of his name that while in Mexico, where he exchanged his gold for greenbacks, although believed to be one of The Express Robbers, there was none bold enough to arrest him.*

Sheriff Glasscock and his posse rode out to Kazy's house late Saturday night and surrounded it. The sheriff ordered his men, "Boys, if you see him, halt him. If he shows fight, shoot him down. If he runs, shoot him in the legs. Catch him at all hazards." The *Mexico Weekly Ledger* continued its account:

In about one-half hour, Glasscock heard a horse "nicker" about one-half a mile off as he thought. Moore and Glasscock then crept toward the noise, went 300 yards down the branch, came to a fence, saw fresh horse tracks; Glasscock got over the fence and got into a thicket, heard the horse snort about 50 yards off in the brush. Glasscock then crawled toward the horse about 90 steps, got upon his knees and saw the back of the horse 40 yards off. Glasscock took off his hat and crept up 20 yards closer. Then he raised up and saw Berry unhitching the horse from a tree. Berry then led his horse aslant toward Glasscock, as Berry now says, to lead him to water. Glasscock cocked both barrels of his gun, ran out about 20 yards, [got] within about 20 feet of Berry and demanded him to halt! Berry started to run. Glasscock shot but aimed too high, which caused the charge to go over Berry's head. He shot again, and 7 buckshot lodged in Berry's left leg below the knee. Berry fell to the ground. When Glasscock got to him, he was trying to get his pistol out, but he could not get it out before Glasscock was on him and snatched it away from him. He then asked Glasscock to shoot him, [saying] that he did not want to live. Glasscock told him no, that he did not want to kill him. He wanted him to have justice. Just then, Moore came up.

What strikes us as strange is that Berry, the "best man in Callaway county," [was] thus taken by one man. Only last Sunday, when Berry was in the hands of Audrain's sheriff, we heard men in Callaway County say that no 20 men could take Berry, and that when Glasscock went out the first time, he did not want to find Berry, &c. they seemed to take pride in Berry's being a bully, and then for Callaway's best man to run at the ominous word "halt!" The fact of the business is that Berry is no coward, but he was taken at a disadvantage, and the persuasive influence of a double-barreled

*breech-loader in the hands of a determined officer will make even the boldest
criminal tremble. Berry, after being caught, even begged the sheriff to shoot
him; but the sheriff, being a humane man, declined to accede to his request.
We take great pride in the fact that our sheriff captured Berry.*

Searching Berry after his capture, Sheriff Glasscock found $2,804. By
Sunday night, the posse and its prisoner had arrived in Mexico. Berry was
placed in a room at the Ringo House, where Dr. Russell attended him.
Berry's seven leg wounds were not thought serious at that time.

Just after midnight on Tuesday morning, Quantrill Raider, veteran and
outlaw James Berry died at the Ringo House from a gangrene infection in
his leg wounds. Mrs. Mary Price Berry, in shock at her husband's death, was
brought to the Ringo House. The day after the robbery, Mrs. Berry had
given birth to daughter Myra Berry at their farm. Now she had six children,
all of whom were dependent solely on her for food and protection. In the
words of the *Mexico Weekly Ledger*, "What ever he may have done, his wife
and children still cling to him as a tender love."

Prior to his death, Berry confessed that he had been involved in the Union
Pacific robbery and that "he was not sorry for it." With several witnesses
present, Berry would say nothing about the other gang members.

Just a few hours prior to Berry's death, his aged mother had died. James
Berry was buried next to his mother in Liberty Church Yard Cemetery,
about three miles northwest of Shamrock, Missouri.

Two mysteries remain about the Jim Berry story. How was Jim Berry
captured? Relatives and friends of Berry dispute the sheriff's claim. By their
account, Sheriff Glasscock came up behind a sleeping Jim Berry, who was
lying on his side in the shade of a large tree. The sheriff fired a shot at the
sleeping Berry, a horse neighed and the wounded Berry emptied his two
six-shooters in retaliation. Only then, wounded and out of ammunition, was
Berry captured.

Less than one-third of Berry's share of the Union Pacific loot was
recovered—what happened to the other $7,000? Although Berry's home
was searched, the stolen money was not found. Had he been able to hide the
money? Did his wife benefit from this stolen money? Mrs. Berry and the six
children continued to live on the farm for three years after Jim Berry's death.
They had relatives and friends, but it seems very likely that the stolen money
helped them survive.

The Union Pacific money also might have helped Mrs. Berry pay the
passage for her family to come to Fort Benton on the steamboat *Red Cloud*

three years later. On June 10, 1880, Mrs. Berry and her children stepped ashore at Fort Benton after a long trip up the Missouri River.

Mrs. Berry came to Fort Benton to join her pro-secessionist father, Cyrus Price, and brothers, Charles W. and Kyle Price, who had come to Montana Territory in the 1860s to avoid service during the Civil War. Over the years, they had become very successful ranchers. The 1880 census, taken shortly after the Berry family's arrival, recorded Mrs. Berry as keeping house for her father at Ulida, Chestnut Valley, near today's Cascade. In February 1885, daughter Addie Price Berry married Highwood rancher John Harris, one of Montana's legendary open-range ranchers. Their descendants remain in the area today.

Mrs. Mary Berry lived near the Highwood Mountains until 1885, when she married C.B. Houser and moved to Butte. In 1898, Mrs. Mary Houser moved to Kalispell to be near her son, John R. Berry, at the Montana Soldier's Home at Columbia Falls. After his death in 1918, she came to Great Falls to stay with her daughter Mrs. Anne Townsend. Mary died in 1927 and rests today in Riverside Cemetery, Fort Benton, with her father.

Confederate veteran James Berry lived a life packed with adventure—from dashing headlong into Quantrill's Raiders to his outlaw days and, finally, to his violent death. His family survived to become prominent in Montana history.

Chapter 8

THE REBEL CONRAD
FAMILY AT WAR

JAMES, WILLIAM G. AND CHARLES CONRAD

For the Conrad family of the Shenandoah Valley of Virginia, the War for Southern Independence was personal, and it was a family affair. James Warren and Maria Ashby Conrad raised thirteen children on Wapping Plantation near Front Royal. Their plantation consisted of rolling acres of fertile land crowned by a white, two-story, porticoed mansion. Life on their plantation was pleasant and peaceful—greatly aided by the forced labor of their eleven slaves. The two eldest Conrad boys—William George, born on August 3, 1848, and Charles Edward, born on May 2, 1850—grew up in the easy lifestyle and warm hospitality typical of the antebellum South. In the summer of 1861, the Civil War erupted with a vengeance in the Shenandoah Valley, destroying the Conrads' slave-based way of life.

As the war began, Colonel James W. Conrad was called to service with the Virginia State Militia. In 1864, his sons William, only sixteen, and even younger fourteen-year-old Charles joined Company C of Mosby's Regiment, Virginia Cavalry Partisan Rangers. Mosby's Rangers was a force composed of guerrillas who ranged across battle lines, wreaking devastation on Union supply depots, troop installations and communications. The daring escapades of Colonel John S. Mosby, the "Gray Ghost" of the Confederacy, especially behind enemy lines, made him feared and detested by Union forces.

Despite their youth, the Conrad brothers earned a strong reputation with Mosby's men. Young Charles, especially, earned a reputation as one of the bravest men in Mosby's command, often devising innovative tactics in the midst of battle.

Colonel John S. Mosby, the "Gray Ghost" of the Confederacy. *Library of Congress.*

By the fall of 1864, Mosby was successfully disrupting supply lines, intercepting Union couriers and evading Union pursuers by disguising himself and his soldiers in civilian clothing. On September 22, 1864, Union troops executed six of Mosby's men who had been captured out of uniform in Front Royal, Virginia, as well as a seventh captured near Rappahannock.

107

After the executions, a Union soldier pinned a piece of paper to one of the bodies. It read: "This shall be the fate of all Mosby's men."

In retaliation, Mosby executed three Union soldiers by hanging. Two more were shot in the head, and although left for dead, both survived. Two other condemned men managed to escape.

In an exchange of letters in mid-November, Mosby and General Philip Sheridan, commander of Union forces in the Shenandoah Valley, agreed to resume treatment of captives as prisoners of war. This stopped the executions.

On November 18, Mosby defeated Richard R. Blazer's scouts at the Battle of Kabletown. On December 21, Mosby was dining at the home of friends near Rector's Crossroads, Virginia. A shot was fired through a window, and the ball entered his abdomen. He managed to stagger into the bedroom and hide his coat, the only item bearing his rank insignia. The commander of the Union detachment, Major Douglas Frazar of the 13th New York Cavalry, then entered the house. Unaware of Mosby's identity, he inspected the wound and declared it mortal. Although left for dead, Mosby recovered and returned to the war within two months.

After General Lee's surrender, Mosby disbanded his rangers on April 21, 1865, in Salem, Virginia, refusing to surrender formally. Many of his men obtained official parole documents from the Federals and returned to their homes, but Mosby himself traveled southward with a small party of officers to join up with General Joseph E. Johnston's army in North Carolina. Before he reached his fellow Confederates, he learned of Johnston's surrender in a newspaper. Though Mosby was a wanted man, General Grant paroled him at the end of June.

William and Charles Conrad were captured on April 22, 1865, at Winchester, Virginia, and paroled to return to the Shenandoah Valley to join their father. Once there, they found their slaves freed and Wapping Plantation devastated by war and unable to support the large Conrad family. The boys worked locally, with Charles gaining experience as a clerk in a general store, before they moved on to New York. It was here that they learned of opportunities in the West.

In 1868, William and Charles boarded a steamboat at St. Louis bound for the Upper Missouri. Family legend relates that on arrival at Fort Benton, they had just a single silver dollar between them, so they split with William moving on to Helena and Charles remaining in Fort Benton. With Charles's experience, the trading company I.G. Baker & Bro. hired him as a clerk. This firm grew rapidly with business expanding throughout Montana and western Canada. Charles married Blackfoot

Parole signed by young Charles E. Conrad after his surrender at the end of the Civil War.
Fold3.com.

Top: William G. Conrad, one of Montana's "merchant princes." *Progressive Men of Montana*.

Right: Teenage Mosby Raider Charles E. Conrad became a wealthy town builder in Montana. *Progressive Men of Montana*.

woman Sings-in-the-Middle, and before her death, son Charles Edward Conrad Jr. was born.

William Conrad returned from Helena to rejoin his brother, and by 1874, the Conrad brothers had become full partners with I.G. Baker. Based at Fort Benton, I.G. Baker & Co. operated fourteen trading posts scattered throughout "Indian country." When the first contingent of the North-West Mounted Police arrived lost and starving in this harsh and unfamiliar country, Charles Conrad came to their rescue. In gratitude, the Canadian government awarded I.G. Baker & Co. a ten-year contract for supplying the mounted police, until arrival of the Canadian Pacific Railroad a decade later. Operating lucrative trading posts at Fort Macleod and Calgary—with Charles in charge of the Canadian trade and William assuming a leading role in the Montana trade and steamboat operations—the Conrads began to build their fortunes.

As the railroad era dawned on Montana, the Conrad brothers sold their steamboats and shifted their partnership to cattle ranching, mining, real estate and banking. Charles married Alicia Stanford in 1879 and later moved his family to the Flathead Valley, founding the city of Kalispell in 1891. Concerned about the demise of the American bison, he bought fifty bison, the beginning of today's herd at Moise's National Bison Range.

William married Fannie E. Bowen in 1876 and eventually moved his family to the growing town of Great Falls to become one of Montana's foremost business leaders. He invested in ranches, copper and silver mines, railroads, banking and real estate. Politically active as a Democrat, he served in the Montana legislature and came within four votes of being elected to the U.S. Senate. In his later years, he lived in Helena and spent winters in Virginia's Shenandoah Valley. His obituary estimated his wealth at $25 million.

Patriarch James W. Conrad brought his wife and youngest daughter from Virginia to Fort Benton to join their sons in 1879. After a dozen years there, the family moved to Great Falls to live with their daughter, Mrs. F.J. Adams.

The three Conrad Confederate soldiers brought boundless energy and success to Montana Territory. Colonel James W. Conrad passed away on July 17, 1894, and rests at Highland Cemetery in Great Falls. Private Charles E. Conrad died on November 27, 1902, and is interred in Conrad Memorial Cemetery in Kalispell. Private William G. Conrad died on March 6, 1914, at his winter home in Montana Hall, White Post, Virginia, and is buried at Mount Hebron Cemetery in Winchester, Virginia.

Chapter 9

FROM ESCORTING PRESIDENT JEFF DAVIS TO MONTANA'S CONFEDERATE GULCH

JOHN AND PERRY MOORE

When the Civil War erupted in Missouri, the Moore brothers, John T. and Perry J., joined local Confederates in battle in northeastern Missouri. The Moores fought hard until the war ended for them in the Carolinas four years later. Returning together to their home in war-torn Shelby County, the brothers found that their mother and younger siblings had migrated to the western territories to escape the violence in Missouri. The brothers followed to settle on the rugged Montana frontier, where they prospected and mined and, later, built successful ranches.

John Thomas Moore, eldest son of John W. and Eleanor Holliday Moore, was born on April 17, 1841, in Shelby County, Missouri, while younger brother Perry James Moore was born on May 8, 1844. Father John W. Moore died in 1854, leaving his wife and five children on the family farm.

When the Civil War began, elder brother John joined the Confederate army while young Perry remained on the family homestead. In June 1861, twenty-year-old John T. Moore enlisted in Colonel Martin E. Green's regiment of volunteer cavalry in northeastern Missouri. John's enlistment record described him as standing five feet, eleven inches tall with blue eyes, a fair complexion and light hair. A leading secessionist in northeastern Missouri, Colonel Green raised the 1st Northeast Missouri Cavalry Regiment (Confederate) in early July, mustered the regiment in at Knox County and was elected colonel with Lieutenant Colonel Joseph C. Porter and Major Benjamin W. Shacklett serving under him.

The hard-charging Moore brothers (Perry J. Moore, standing; John T. Moore, seated) helped Jeff Davis evade capture and then became successful Montana ranchers. *Montana Historical Society 944-001.*

Colonel Green went on the offensive in northeastern Missouri in August 1861, attempting to scatter Colonel David Moore's 1st Northeast Missouri Home Guard Regiment (Union). Green's much larger force of two thousand men and a battery of two cannon struck Moore at Athens, Missouri. Colonel Moore's men had received Springfield rifles and bayonets, while the Confederates had few rounds for their cannon, were poorly equipped and trained, and were armed primarily with shotguns and squirrel rifles. Private John Moore and the other secessionists attacked, and after initial success, their advance faltered as they approached through a cornfield. Major Shacklett was wounded, and his demoralized men began falling back. Colonel Moore commanded his men to fix bayonets and charge. Their counterattack routed the Confederates into a headlong retreat.

The 1st Northeast Missouri Cavalry became part of the Second District/Second Division, commanded by Col. Green, in the Missouri State Guard under General Sterling Price. Colonel Green's men engaged in a number of skirmishes and engagements after the debacle at Athens. During this period, they gained improved training, arms and equipment.

Now part of Price's army, Colonel Green's men left northern Missouri with the Missouri State Guard. In mid-September 1861, the 1st Northeast Missouri participated in a successful attack on Lexington, Missouri, where it overwhelmed Union forces and captured Union commander Colonel James A. Mulligan. From September 13 to the 20th, General Price's army of 15,000 men laid siege to the river town of Lexington, defended by just 3,500 men primarily of the 23rd Illinois Infantry. On September 18, Price mounted a major assault on Mulligan's heavily fortified defensive works. After that assault failed, Confederate artillery pounded Mulligan's men. On the twentieth, elements of Price's army used hemp bales soaked in the nearby Missouri River to act as mobile breastworks to work their way up the river bluffs toward Mulligan's position. By early afternoon, Mulligan was forced to surrender. Light Confederate losses totaled just 25 killed and 72 wounded, while the Federals lost 39 killed, 120 wounded and over 3,000 prisoners of war.

Shortly after the Battle of Lexington, Private John Moore was taken ill with measles and left at Johnstown, south of Kansas City. Within six weeks, Private Moore was taken prisoner and held in captivity in St. Louis until about mid-April 1862. Then, while being taken on a steamboat from St. Louis across the Mississippi River to the Union prison at Alton, Illinois, he escaped.

By May, Private John Moore had returned to Missouri to join Colonel Porter's 1st Northeast Missouri Cavalry along with his brother Perry.

In the spring of 1862, the fighting between Union forces and Confederate bushwhackers in Shelby County and adjoining Knox County exploded. Colonel John M. Glover of the 3rd Missouri Cavalry, commanding Union forces in northeastern Missouri, ordered his men to suppress the bushwhackers. The conflict extended to civilians as well in the guerrilla warfare environment. On April 10, Colonel Glover issued Special Order No. 30:

> *In every case within your reach where the rebels take a dollar's worth of property of any kind from a Union man or family, do you take at least twice as much in value from rebels in the vicinity (from parties who took the goods if you can identify them) and hold it for security for return of the property...You will forthwith levy an assessment and collect it from the wealthy secessionists in the vicinity sufficient to comfortably support the families of those members of the M.S.M.* [the Union's Missouri State Militia] *who were killed by the rebels, and see that they are comfortably supported by this means until further orders.*

Two days later, enclosing a list of sixty-five names of men in the region, Colonel Glover ordered Captain John F. Benjamin of Shelbyville to capture the men, induce them to try to escape and then shoot them. Into this environment of total warfare in May 1862, eighteen-year-old Perry J. Moore enlisted in Colonel Joseph C. Porter's Regiment, joining his older brother John. Perry was described as six feet tall with gray eyes, a fair complexion and light hair. Hundreds of men from Shelby County belonged to Porter's command, while at least one hundred belonged to Union forces arrayed against them. Porter's men lived off the country, foraging as they went, and served as their own quartermaster and commissary.

In guerrilla fashion, Porter's men roamed the countryside until July 18, when Union forces from Newark attacked in a bloody engagement ending in about 108 casualties for Federal troops and just 20 for the Rebels. Despite this initial victory, arrival of Union reinforcements forced Colonel Porter to retreat. By July 19, Porter's men, including the Moore brothers, had fought a battle and marched sixty-five miles in less than twenty-four hours. They had not eaten in thirty-six hours and were exhausted, yet the Federals kept the pressure on them. When pursuing Federal commander Colonel John McNeil was asked where Porter was, he replied, "How can I tell? He may be at any point within 100 miles. He runs like a deer and doubles like a fox. I hear that he crossed the North Missouri, going south, to-day, but I would not be surprised if he fired on our pickets before morning."

Ten days later, on July 28, Porter's harassed men suffered another defeat from troops of Colonel Odon Guitar, a snarling Missouri Unionist "tiger." Retreating again, Porter managed to evade. He continued to build up his force until by early August, it numbered three thousand men. Feeling confident, Porter occupied Kirksville, county seat of Adair County in northeastern Missouri, and set up defenses. Union forces under Colonel McNeil, a savage fighter, attacked on August 6. McNeil sent ten men to reconnoiter Porter's defensive positions in the town. The scouting force charged into the center of town, around the square and through the streets, learning that every house was a Trojan horse and every garden fence an ambuscade, while the courthouse was a fortress with its lower windows fortified and filled with sharpshooters. After receiving the fire from one thousand shotguns, rifles and revolvers but losing just one man, the cavalrymen rode to safety with their report.

As the fight began, Porter's fatal miscalculation became clear—he had no artillery, while Colonel McNeil had five cannon. Methodically, the Union artillery tore the wood frame "Trojan horse" houses to fragments and crushed brick walls as if they were eggshells. The Confederates fell back. Slowly the Federals advanced under cover of their artillery yet out of range of Confederate shotguns. Demoralized by the artillery fire, the Confederates began to give way. The Federals skirmished slightly and then stood off before battering the Confederates to pieces with their artillery. Finally, the Federals charged, creating panic among the Rebels and driving the whole force in terror from the field.

Private John T. Moore later wrote an account of the capture and execution of Colonel Frisby McCulloch, CSA, two days after the Battle of Kirksville. Colonel McCulloch was charged, tried and sentenced to death as a bushwhacker, even though he was captured wearing a regular Confederate uniform and carrying letters authorizing him to recruit troops. The colonel and twenty-six of his men were sentenced for execution for having broken previous prisoner paroles. Colonel McCulloch asked the privilege of giving the word to fire, and his request was granted. So, when all was ready, he gave the word for his own execution and that of his men, saying, "May God forgive you for this cold-blooded murder. Aim at the heart. Fire!" A second volley was necessary.

The Battle of Kirksville helped consolidate Union dominance and ended most bushwhacking in northeastern Missouri. It destroyed Porter's regiment, which disintegrated and scattered, suffering as many as 200 killed, 400 wounded and 250 prisoners compared to the Union's 8 killed and 33 wounded. With this catastrophic defeat, Porter disbanded his regiment. His surviving men broke into small groups to escape, with many survivors deserting and heading west.

Fleeing from Kirksville, the Moore brothers with a young man named John B. Suttle dressed themselves in civilian clothes; crossed the Mississippi River in a skiff a few miles below Quincy, Illinois; walked out into the country a few miles; boarded a train; and rode on to Madison, Indiana, on the Ohio River. From there, they made their way by foot into Kentucky and spent the first night with Jesse James's grandfather John M. James. The Moore brothers planned to continue moving south to join a new unit.

Confederate general Braxton Bragg had abandoned Kentucky, moving out of the state and leaving it wholly in Union hands. As the Moores proceeded south, they passed on from one Southern sympathizer to another until they reached the home of a man named Pendleton, who had sons in Colonel John Hunt Morgan's 2nd Kentucky Cavalry Regiment. He advised them to remain quiet and wait for an expected raid by Morgan.

After waiting in vain for some weeks, the Moores joined a man who was moving north with beef and got as far as Indiana and Illinois. From there, they returned to Kentucky, and finally, after many hairbreadth escapes and traveling by night and hiding by day, they crossed the Cumberland River and joined the 9th Kentucky Cavalry, under command of Colonel W.C.P. Breckenridge. The 9th Kentucky was assigned to the Second Brigade of Brigadier General John Hunt Morgan's division. With this command, they joined Bragg's army and continued southward, participating in the retreat from Murfreesboro to Chattanooga and skirmishing on the way before the Battle of Chickamauga on September 19–20, 1863.

At this time, Perry Moore became ill with typhoid fever and was sent to a hospital in Georgia, where he remained for six weeks before rejoining his regiment in Alabama. The 9th Kentucky reunited with General Bragg's army in time to take part in the Battle of Missionary Ridge on November 25, when they fought almost every day for thirty days.

The 9th Kentucky spent the winter in scout and picket duty at Tunnel Hill with the Army of Tennessee camped at Dalton, Georgia. While intercepting a baggage train, Perry Moore was shot in the left knee. After eight weeks in a hospital, he rejoined his regiment in the spring of 1864, and from that time he and the 9th Kentucky were in heavy action under cavalry commander General Joseph Wheeler, advancing and retreating but always fighting during the march from Dalton to Atlanta.

On May 7, 1864, Union general William T. Sherman began his Atlanta Campaign. The 9th Kentucky fought and helped defeat General John W. Geary's division of Hooker's Corps at Dug Gap and fought engagements at Snake Creek Gap, Cassville, Cartersville, Altoona, Marietta, Roseville Factory, Peach Tree Creek and finally the Battle of Atlanta. On about May 10, the 9th Kentucky crossed the Chattahoochee River, marching north with Wheeler's Corp to destroy Sherman's railroad communications.

During the Atlanta Campaign, on July 31, 1864, a Union raiding force led by Brigadier General George Stoneman Jr. attempted to seize Andersonville Prison to free Union prisoners held there. The 9th Kentucky engaged in battle at Sunshine Church, leading to the capture of Stoneman.

The 9th Kentucky marched through Tennessee to Virginia to join in the Battle of Saltville, where Confederates defeated General Stephen Burbridge. Constantly on the move with running engagements, the 9th Kentucky returned to Atlanta as Sherman began his March to the Sea on November 16, 1864. Over the next several months and into the spring of 1865, the 9th Kentucky, part of the Kentucky Cavalry Brigade, tried to harass Sherman's army in many engagements.

The 9th Kentucky fought its way through the southeast to Bentonville, North Carolina. That major battle was the last engagement for the Moore brothers. The Battle of Bentonville was the last major action of the Civil War in which a Confederate army was able to mount a tactical offensive. It was the largest ever fought in North Carolina and was the only major attempt to defeat the powerful Union army of General Sherman during its march through the Carolinas to the sea in the spring of 1865.

Under the exceptionally capable General Joseph E. Johnston, Confederate forces fought well at Bentonville, but they could not overcome the overwhelming Union strength and the heavy casualties suffered during the battle. Just over one month later, General Johnston surrendered to General Sherman at Bennett Place, North Carolina.

After Bentonville, the 9th Kentucky was ordered to join the military escort for fleeing Confederate president Jefferson Davis. While most Americans believed the war was over and the Confederacy was disintegrating, Davis still held out hope. On April 2, President Davis with a cadre of his advisors and cabinet members fled from the capital at Richmond to Danville in southern Virginia. Over the next month, the shrinking Confederate government continued to move southward, pursued by Federal forces. On April 11, the regiment moved on to Raleigh, North Carolina, where it heard of the surrender of General Robert E. Lee. On April 18, the 9th Kentucky Cavalry joined President Davis and his cabinet to provide military escort for them. At Charlotte, North Carolina, the party halted a few days pending negotiations between Generals Joseph E. Johnston and Sherman.

The president's party and its military escort left Charlotte and moved on to Petersburg, South Carolina, on the Savannah River on May 8. At Abbeville, South Carolina, the last Confederate council of war was held. At that meeting, President Jefferson Davis met with General John C. Breckinridge, General Braxton Bragg and five brigade commanders: Generals George G. Dibrell, Samuel W. Ferguson, John C. Vaughn and Basil W. Duke and Colonel W.C.P. Breckinridge of the 9th Kentucky, who was then commanding the Kentucky Cavalry Brigade. At this council, the members decided that the struggle was hopeless and that any effort to reach the Trans-Mississippi Department would only fail. President Davis cast the only dissenting vote but ultimately accepted the resolution.

There, at the Savannah River, President Davis authorized compensation for his advisors from the remaining Confederate treasury. In addition, the Moore brothers and the other soldiers of the military escort were paid $28 each in specie for their services. The soldiers received an estimated $108,000, part of the last money paid out by the Confederate government from its depleted treasury. Perry Moore retained $1 of this payment for many years as a souvenir of his role in the end of the Confederacy.

The Davis military escort was then told to surrender to pursuing Union soldiers. On May 10, 1865, the 9th Kentucky Regiment marched to Washington, Georgia, and surrendered to Union forces. That same morning, the 1st Wisconsin and 4th Michigan Cavalries captured President Davis and his party at Irwinville, North Carolina. Among the stories in the 1st U.S. Volunteer Infantry's *Frontier Scout* was this apocryphal account of the capture of the president of the Confederacy.

> *Jeff Davis in Petticoats. Grand climax of a bloody farce! Jeff. Davis stealing away in his wife's crinoline! But he was so spurred on by fear he forgot his spurs. His heels were his ruin. They did their duty, but were not properly rigged. He, like the "nigger" in one of Lincoln's stories, struck for the words, but got stopped by the last ditch. What pride those heroes who have lost a limb in his service must feel! What numbers of rat-terriers and bull-dogs will bear his name! Who will replenish his wife's shattered wardrobe, and sew up her torn linen? Jeff Davis running like a scared chicken to hide himself in the brush! Who won't be proud to have been "secech"? Who won't have for their coat of arms a petticoat and spur with a chicken Rampant!*

This popular Yankee image depicts President Jefferson Davis at his capture dressed in woman's clothing and given away by his boots. In fact, he was wearing only his wife, Varina's, large shawl. *Author's collection.*

On May 22, 1865, John and Perry Moore subscribed to the oath of allegiance to the United States, and their war was over. The U.S. government furnished transportation for the paroled 9th Kentucky soldiers, and the Moore brothers returned to their home in Shelby County, Missouri. There, they learned that their mother and siblings had moved west the previous year. The message they received was: "Please tell my boys, if they make it home from the War, that we've gone West to the Mines."

In 1864, because of severe conditions in Missouri, Mrs. Eleanor Moore, her daughter Nancy, her son Sanford and twelve-year-old Willie Johns, son of Mrs. Moore's stepdaughter, left their family farm to join a wagon train heading for Montana Territory. Despite being widowed and fifty-seven years of age, Mrs. Moore bravely led her family westward. The Moore family drove their wagon and four milk cows and finally, one year later, arrived in Virginia City with the family intact and two surviving cows. After spending 1865 in Virginia City, the following spring, the Moore family followed a stampede of prospectors to Diamond City in Confederate Gulch on the Missouri River, where rich strikes had been located on Montana Bar. There, Mrs. Moore opened a boardinghouse to support her family.

To John and Perry, the "West" was a lot of territory. Apparently, the two parted to find their separate ways to Colorado in searching for their family. John Moore moved on to Nebraska and was hired as a "bullwhacker" to cross the plains to Denver. Not finding his mother in the Colorado mines, he came to Montana the following spring with a large cattle outfit, arriving at Diamond City on August 10, 1866, to finally reunite with his family.

In July 1865, Perry Moore started for Montana Territory when he was hired to drive an ox team from Nebraska City to Denver. He wintered over there and, in the spring of 1866, joined a wagon train to Montana. His first destination in the territory was Bannack, arriving in July to try his hand at prospecting. From there, he pushed on to Last Chance Gulch and finally on to Diamond City to reunite with his family. Mrs. Eleanor Moore died in Diamond City in November 1868.

In Diamond City, Perry joined brothers John and Sanford to engage in hauling timber to the mines in the gulches in the area. They employed a number of teams and men, and after two years, the Moore brothers moved east to the Smith River Valley. There, they bought a sawmill in the Dry Range country on the lower Smith River and furnished lumber to Diamond City and the military post at Fort Logan.

The Moore brothers also ran a small herd of cattle in the Smith River Valley. Perry Moore was one of the first arrivals at White Sulphur Springs when that town was founded. The brothers owned and operated a ranch in the Smith River Valley, twenty-five miles from White Sulphur Springs.

In 1871, the onset of an early winter caused some concern for their cattle, and hearing of open range in the Musselshell Valley, John drove the cattle there while Perry and Sanford were in California on a horse-buying expedition. Later that spring, the cattle were returned to the Smith River Ranch, with John maintaining operations there. In 1872, Perry and Sanford decided to remain on the Musselshell. Later, in the 1880s, Sanford took up freighting operations.

In leaving the Smith River area, Perry took up a homestead of 160 acres in addition to 400 acres of desert land along the Musselshell River in central Montana near the later town of Two Dot, where he lived the rest of his life. Over the years, Perry greatly expanded his holdings until his ranch encompassed 12,000 acres. He became one of the leading landowners and for many years was a prominent sheep man in central Montana. The Moore ranch expanded into raising hay, grain, cattle and sheep. In his later years, Perry spent much of his time in California.

A lifelong Democrat, Perry Moore was elected narrowly to the Fourteenth Territorial Legislature in 1885, representing Meagher County. He served as school trustee at Two Dot for many years, was a past master of the Diamond City Lodge of Masons at White Sulphur Springs, a member of Harlowton Chapter No. 22 Royal Arch Masons and belonged to Loyal Lodge No. 27, Knights of Pythias, at Two Dot. He was a major stockholder in the State Bank of Two Dot. Perry Moore was a member of the United Confederate Veterans and the Nathan Bedford Forrest Camp No. 1390 of Helena, Montana.

On August 17, 1881, Perry Moore married Miss Nellie Robertson, who was born in 1859 at Prescott, Ontario. Her father, George F. Robertson, had come to Canada from Scotland. Perry and Nellie Moore had four children: Nellie, the eldest, widow of physician and surgeon Dr. H.B. Tice; sons Perry James Jr. and George Fulton; and another daughter, Margaret Moore.

Proud Confederate veteran Perry J. Moore passed away on August 16, 1921, in Lewistown and is interred at Mayn Cemetery in White Sulphur Springs.

John Moore remained at Diamond City until 1870, operating the sawmill business with his brothers and William H. Sutherlin, later publisher of the *Rocky Mountain Husbandman*.

During his residence at Diamond City, John Moore married Miss Irene Lewis, daughter of G.S. Lewis, of New York, who came to Montana in 1866. In 1870, Moore moved to a three-thousand-acre ranch near the site of old Camp Baker at the mouth of Sheep Creek. There, he had a fine ranch with

Mining boomtown Diamond City in Confederate Gulch, 1866. *Montana Historical Society 946-724.*

barns, sheds and other outbuildings, as well as an excellent residence. He raised cattle and horses on a large scale, with shorthorn cattle and draught horses being his favorite breeds.

In their later years, John and Irene Moore lived in Long Beach, California. There, in 1926, John wrote his "Memoirs," published on July 19, 1926, by the Montana Newspaper Association in Montana's weekly newspapers, including the *Judith Gap Journal*. John Moore's account bypassed the early years back in Missouri and the Civil War and focused on the early times as pioneers in Meagher County. The Moore memoir gave a picture of the fun, as well as some of the hardships, of life in Montana in the late 1860s and '70s.

Among his many anecdotes, John Moore wrote movingly about his dear wife, Irene:

> *On August 31, 1869, I was married to Irene Lewis of Diamond City, the dearest little girl that ever crossed the plains in a covered wagon. She passed away on August 14th, 1921, in Long Beach. We had lived together 52*

years and I do not think there was ever two people in Montana that lived together that long and thought more of each other than we did.

He wrote of the arrival of the military in the Smith River Valley:

In the winter of 1869 and '70, a company of United States soldiers came over and built a temporary post on the Moore ranch that they called Camp Baker. In the summer of that year they moved ten miles up the river and built Fort Logan. The Moore boys furnished all the lumber for the fort.

And he wrote of some hardships during the early years:

The winter of 1871 and 1872 was one of the hardest winters we ever had in Montana. On the 22nd day of November 1871, the thermometer dropped from 21 above to 40 below in less than one hour. A man by the name of G.F. Snelling, one of the commissioners of Meagher County, went out to look for a cow and was [found] frozen to death two days later 20 miles from home. He had a bunch of fine splinters in his hand, which showed he had been trying to light a fire, as they were partly burned, but he had no more matches.

We had zero and below weather from the 22nd of November until the middle of February. The snow got to be about three feet deep all over Smith River valley. About the first of January, W.S. Sweet and Bill Gordon moved their band of about 600 cattle from Smith River to the Musselshell valley, where there was no snow.

About the first of February, G.S. Lewis, father of Len Lewis, Ed Sayre and I started for the Musselshell with 376 head of cattle, got as far as the Dogy ranch, bought a small stack of hay from Jim Brewer and stayed there two days in a storm and fed the hay to the cattle; then drove on to Fort Harvey, got there the 13th, turned the cattle loose on bare ground...The 14th of February the Chinook came and took all the snow off the ground in the Smith River valley, and we had no bad weather after that. The latter part of March, Mr. Lewis and I went back after our cattle and found them all within five miles of where we left them. We drove 375 head back to Smith River, having lost one head from the time they left home till they got back.

John Moore wrote about the colorful origins of the town of White Sulphur Springs:

In 1873, Jim Brewer built a log cabin at the Springs, cleaned out the spring, built a house over it, charged the boys 75 cents each for a bath, sold whiskey and ran one hell of a place. In '74, it got to be quite a health resort. The neighbors would gather from all over the valley and run horses, drink, gamble, fight and have a good time. On July 4th, 1874, a big crowd from all over the valley were there and had one grand time. Brewer set up a big tent for the ladies to dress in. Sanford Moore was riding a little buckskin horse that was chuck full of buck. He tied him to the rack and went into the house. Jess Edwards, a professional gambler who was known all over the territory as "6 Fingered Jess," got on Sanford's buckskin and rode up to the race track. When the race was over, the boys all started running their horses back to the house and Jess's mount turned loose bucking, threw old Jess off, tore off nearly all his clothes, got the saddle under him, ran into the guy ropes of the tent, turned it over and left the ladies all standing there looking like a lot of bathing beauties. However, nothing like that kept us from having lots of fun, and that was what we were looking for.

Private Moore remained active in his community and a proud member of the United Confederate Veterans and the Nathan Bedford Forrest Camp No. 1390 in Helena. Just months after his memoirs were published, John T. Moore, Confederate veteran and Montana pioneer, passed away at age eight-five on December 1, 1926, in Long Beach. He rests today in Mayn Cemetery in White Sulphur Springs.

Chapter 10

A YOUNG CONFEDERATE
IN WAR AND PEACE

PRIVATE SHIRLEY ASHBY

As the Civil War ended, Confederate private Shirley C. Ashby hung his arms on a nearby tree and surrendered on April 20, 1865, at Millwood, Virginia, near his home in the Shenandoah Valley after his 6th Virginia Cavalry Regiment disbanded. He signed a parole of allegiance to the United States and began planning his future in the West.

Shirley Carter Ashby was born to George William and Phoebe Carter Ashby in Mason County, western Virginia, on August 19, 1842. When Shirley was two, his family moved east—first to Fauquier and then to Clarke County. There, in the Shenandoah Valley, he was raised on the modest Ashby farm with just one household slave and a baby.

On September 22, 1862, twenty-year-old Shirley Ashby enlisted in Company D, 1st Virginia Cavalry (later designated the 6th). He was five feet, eleven inches tall with a light complexion, light hair and dark eyes. Virginia's 6th Cavalry had been organized in November 1861 at Manassas as Virginia prepared for war—and war the 6th got, fighting almost continuously with Robertson's, "Grumble" Jones's, Lunsford L. Lomax's and William H.F. Payne's brigades in Major General Fitzhugh Lee's division of General Robert E. Lee's Army of Northern Virginia.

The 6th Virginia Cavalry fought in General Stonewall Jackson's Shenandoah Valley Campaign and in battles at Second Manassas (Bull Run), Brandy Station, Upperville, Fairfield, Bristoe, Mine Run, Gettysburg, the Wilderness, Todd's Tavern, Spotsylvania, Haw's Shop and Cold Harbor. The regiment went on to take part in Lieutenant General Jubal Early's

One of the Confederacy's "fightinest" regiments, the 6th Virginia Cavalry. *Library of Congress.*

Shenandoah Valley operations in 1864 and the Appomattox Campaign. Only three men of the 6th surrendered on April 9, 1865, at Appomattox, as most of the Confederate cavalry, including the 6th Virginia, cut through Federal lines and only later disbanded. The "Fighting 6th" fought in an incredible two hundred battles and engagements during the Civil War.

When Private Ashby's war was over, he headed west. He first traveled to St. Louis, where he attended commercial college and worked as clerk on a steamboat. In September 1866, he came down with cholera during an epidemic in St. Louis and was advised to go "to the mountains" for recovery. At that time, Ashby met prominent steamboat man Captain D.S. Carter, a close friend of former Confederate soldier Captain Nicholas Wall, manager of the giant Diamond R Overland Freighting Company in Montana Territory. Carter advised young Ashby to go to Montana.

Thus, Shirley Ashby joined his older brother Captain Wirth Ashby aboard the steamboat *Nile* for the fifty-nine-day trip up the Missouri River. The steamer's clerk was sick, so the captain hired Shirley Ashby to take over this important job. On landing at Fort Benton on June 12, 1867, Ashby discharged the two hundred tons of cargo and settled with consignees. He received $500 for his services, a very welcome sum to add to the $5 then in his pocket.

One of Virginia's young Rebel soldiers, Shirley Ashby. *Norma Ashby*.

The clerk's job led to employment by Fort Benton commission merchants B.A. Melton, John Taylor and Kinzel at a salary of $300 per month plus board, which, at that time in the bustling river port town, was $15 per week in gold dust. Unable to find a room in Fort Benton, Ashby slept in a warehouse with a candle box and boot tops for a pillow.

A short time later, merchant I.G. Baker hired Ashby at an increased salary to work for his trading company and allowed Ashby to board at the Baker home (today, this historic wood-covered adobe house is open to the public on Front Street in Fort Benton).

In this position, on July 1, 1867, Ashby became the last man to hand mail to General Thomas Francis Meagher, who was spending his last afternoon using the back of the Baker store for an office. Just hours later, Meagher fell from the steamboat *G.A. Thomson* into the Missouri River, never to be seen again.

The Overland Hotel was the only hotel in Fort Benton at this time. In the fall of 1867, after becoming commander of the Department of Missouri, famed Union general Philip H. Sheridan made an inspection trip to Montana Territory. Arriving in Fort Benton from Helena to await steamboat transportation downriver to Camp Cooke, there was no room at the Overland, so Baker and Ashby called on the general and invited him to stay at the Baker home. Ashby offered his room, and the general accepted. Ashby later wrote about this event:

> *I was a Confederate who had been fighting for years in Virginia against this same man. There were times when we were going ahead of one another, with a particular desire that the one in the rear catch the other. How many times this might have occurred, I am not at liberty to say, and it seemed strange that this man, who had been my enemy only a short time before, should be compelled to accept my hospitality. Phil did not know, and I did not enlighten him, that I was one of the boys who had caused him to make history in the valley of the Shenandoah. I remember his saying, "There is old Virginia, her glory has departed."*

The following year, General Winfield Scott Hancock, a Union hero at Gettysburg, came to Fort Benton, and Ashby once again graciously gave up his room. In the summer of 1868, the U.S. Department of the Interior issued an order allowing only two parties to be licensed to go out and trade with the Indians in Choteau County. This order resulted from incidents in which Indians had come to Fort Benton to trade robes and conduct business with the Blackfeet Indian Agency. During trading, some Indians would begin drinking and sell their robes and furs for whiskey. Several incidents occurred in which Fort Benton toughs would shoot or hang visiting Indians. In an attempt to lessen the chances for whiskey trading and reduce violence, the trading posts were moved some distance from Fort Benton.

Montana Union (U) and Confederate (C) Civil War veterans. *Top row, left to right*: Colonel G.I. Reiche (U), Shirley Ashby (C), Captain William Schmidt (unknown). *Front row, left to right*: T.H. Clineschmidt (U), Felix Ingram (C) and an unidentified man. *Montana Historical Society*.

As Shirley Ashby later wrote:

> *The country north of Ft. Benton was divided as follows: I.G. Baker and Brother received a license to trade in the Indian country north with the Bloods and the North Blackfoot, on the Marias River. Another license was issued to I.G. Baker and Co. to trade at the mouth of People's Creek on the Milk River (Fort Browning), where Chas W. Price could trade with the Gros Ventres and Assinaboines. The other license was issued to the Northwest Fur Company, James Hubbell, and John Riplinger, managers. They located on the Teton about a mile or two from the town of Choteau.* [About this same time, the Indian Agency was moved from Fort Benton to this same location.]
>
> *Baker and Brother employed Roche de Rouche, a Frenchman, to manage and interpret the Trading Post on the Marias, at a large and handsome salary.*
>
> *The loading of a large number of teams was left to me. Of course I saw to it that the goods were loaded in good shape, and everything was gotten ready, the wagons in the corral, teamsters hired, and cattle in shape to move.*

Adapting quickly to the rugged Montana frontier, Ashby boldly established two Indian trading posts: Fort Ashby, on the upper Marias River, where he traded with Blackfoot Indians, and the other at Frenchman Creek, thirty-five miles above old Fort Peck, where he traded with Assiniboine Indians. The success of both posts led to Ashby being named partner in the I.G. Baker Company. He later sold his partnership in 1870 to his cousins William G. and Charles Conrad for a substantial profit and moved on to Helena.

In Helena, Ashby married Mrs. Emma Withers Guy of Huntsville, Missouri, in August 1876; served as Lewis and Clark County assessor; and prospered in real estate, insurance and the agricultural implement business. He acquired stock in the Helena National Bank in 1890 and became president two years later. As his fortune grew, he built a nineteen-room Queen Anne–style mansion for his family in 1886. Located at 642 Dearborn Street on Helena's west side, this mansion grandly stands today in its original historic setting.

During the financial panic of 1893, Ashby lost his fortune; he was able to save his fine home only because it was in Emma Ashby's name. A decade later, the mansion was sold to the family of Senator Thomas C. Carter, and the Ashby family moved to a more modest home in Helena. Also in 1903, Shirley Ashby was appointed Montana adjutant general, the state's senior military officer.

Shirley C. Ashby served proudly as adjutant in the Nathan Bedford Forrest Camp of the United Confederate Veterans in Helena. In 1913, Governor Sam V. Steward appointed ten Confederates, including Ashby, and an equal number of Union veterans to represent Montana at the fiftieth anniversary commemoration of the Battle of Gettysburg. (Appropriately, Private Ashby's 6th Virginia Cavalry had fought at Gettysburg). Civil War veteran Shirley Ashby passed away on June 2, 1924, and rests today at Forestvale Cemetery in Helena.

Chapter 11

FROM PLANTATION BOYHOOD
TO CONFEDERATE SOLDIER:

"SANDBAR" FRANK D. BROWN

John Francis Dean "Sandbar" Brown, a man of many names and adventures, fought for the South in the Civil War and left an indelible mark when he came to Montana Territory at war's end. Born on November 24, 1845, to socially and politically prominent parents in Bedford City, Nelson County, Virginia, Frank's great-grandfathers, Benjamin Harrison and Richard Henry Lee, both signed the Declaration of Independence.

Young John Brown was reared on Montezuma Plantation in the rolling hills of Virginia's Piedmont, and he little realized he was destined for remarkable pioneer experiences in the West. In 1850, John's father was a civil engineer, and the family owned one household slave, Sarah Read, age thirty.

Brown's father died in 1859, and two years later, in June 1861, fifteen-year-old John F. Brown enlisted in the Confederate army. In November 1861, Private Brown was assigned to the Quartermaster Department under Captain James R. McClelland. The following April, he transferred to the Confederate War Department, where he served as orderly for his cousin Secretary of War James A. Seddon.

In early 1863, Private Brown joined Company D, 25th Virginia Infantry Battalion, also known as the Richmond Battalion and the City Battalion. The 25th provided local defense for the Richmond area and was on constant guard duty throughout the city, then the capital of the Confederacy. With the Union controlling much of coastal Virginia and North Carolina, inland cities like Richmond were starving. Much of the cropland in central Virginia and the Shenandoah Valley went unattended as soldiers left their farms to fight

Confederate secretary of war James A. Seddon. *Library of Congress.*

for their country and slaves emancipated themselves. The rail system was overtaxed from supporting the fighting forces, and food that did make it to Richmond was sold by merchants and speculators at exorbitant prices.

With the ranks of police depleted, order broke down. In the words of historian Michael Chesson, "Wartime Richmond had become a city of strangers and camp followers, some with criminal intent." The Battle of Sharpsburg (Antietam), during General Robert E. Lee's first invasion of Northern soil, had ended badly for the Confederacy, providing a wake-up call for those who thought the war would soon end. The winter leading into 1863 had gone badly in Richmond, with a devastating explosion at a major ordnance plant in March killing forty-five female employees followed by heavy snow and ice and a breakdown in the city's waterworks.

On March 27, Confederate president Jefferson Davis blundered when he called on Confederates everywhere to spend the day in prayer and fasting. A clerk in the War Department wrote, "Fasting in the midst of famine! May God save this people!" Angry women took to the streets, protesting against hoarders and grain speculators. Women from within the city and nearby counties descended on the Confederate capital. The situation rapidly escalated into violence. The Richmond Battalion deployed to protect the capitol. With President Davis on the scene, in the face of threats of troop commanders to fire on the rioters, the women fled before shots were fired. Artillery was brought into position to defend the capitol and business district. The Confederate army was placed on alert, but a second day of demonstrations was called off, and the authorities rounded up riot leaders.

Secretary of War Seddon pleaded with city newspapers to suppress the story and telegraph operators to remain silent, yet the suppression did not work. Brief but clear reports of "Bread Riot" appeared in print, and city residents, both white and black, knew what had happened.

In September 1863, Private John Brown was discharged from the 25th Battalion and immediately reenlisted as a Confederate marine. The Confederate States Marine Corps (CSMC), a branch of the Confederate States Navy, was established in March 1861. By September 1862, its manpower was authorized at 1,026 enlisted men. The organization of the corps had begun at Montgomery, Alabama, and was completed at Richmond. Throughout the war, the CSMC headquarters and main training facilities were located at Camp Beall on Drewry's Bluff near Richmond and at the Gosport Shipyard in Norfolk.

The CSMC was modeled after the U.S. Marine Corps, which had already established itself as a disciplined organization. The CSMC never approached its authorized manpower and in October 1864 listed only 539 officers and men. CSMC units were stationed at naval bases and with garrisons at shore fortifications like Fort Fisher in North Carolina. Marines served on Confederate warships such as the ocean raider CSS *Alabama*. In mid-1862, the CSMC was broken into squad-sized units and dispersed throughout the South and aboard Confederate ships.

Private Brown served with a CSMC unit on the steamer *Powhatan*, commanded by Lieutenant William Severe. The *Powhatan* served as a tender to the ironclad *Virginia* until its officers destroyed the boat at the surrender of Richmond in April 1865. At that time, Brown's marine regiment assembled at Drewry's Bluff on the James River, where the men surrendered to the 15th Pennsylvania Infantry and were taken to Petersburg for parole.

About this time, Brown dropped "John" from his name because of his distaste for the Union army's marching song "John Brown's Body." Defeated but unbowed, Private Frank D. Brown would remain an unreconstructed Confederate for the rest of his life.

The Civil War brought desolation to the Southland, and under these conditions, the young veteran of the Confederacy decided to leave Virginia and seek his fortune in the West. At the time of his parole, Private Brown was given rations and transportation to St. Louis, Missouri. He later wrote a short account of his decision:

I was a young Confederate soldier after Lee's surrender. I went to St. Louis and entered the employ of the American Fur Company and arrived at Fort Union…Of an adventurous disposition, I went out of the service of the company the March following, with two half-breed Frenchmen, to trap beaver and otter on the lower tributaries of the Yellowstone. I engaged in this work more or less profitably, but being bothered by the Sioux, went over to the Judith and Musselshell, where I traded at Fort Hawley and Fort Benton.

During his long life, Brown gave varying accounts of his activities in his early years in Montana. On his arrival at St. Louis, the Northwest Fur Company hired him and put him on the *Hattie May*, the first company steamboat to make its way up the Missouri River to the Montana mining frontier in 1865. His claim of employment with the American Fur Company no doubt blurred over the years. During the summer of 1865, the Upper Missouri operations of that company had been purchased by the Northwest Fur Company; thus, Brown likely was hired and received passage up the river as an employee of the new company.

Reaching Fort Union on September 17, 1865, Frank Brown proceeded to Fort Benton, arriving in December of that year. In Montana Territory, he worked as wolfer, wood hawk, fur trapper, scout and placer miner on the Yellowstone, Musselshell, Judith and Missouri Rivers. In 1872, he was a scout under Colonel Eugene Baker at Fort Ellis on an expedition to protect surveyors of the first Northern Pacific survey up the Yellowstone River. In Brown's words:

Felix Ingram and myself were to furnish meat to the survey outfit of Colonel [Ferdinand V.] Hayden. We had our first brush with the Indians on a slough—an enclosed piece of land opposite the mouth of Pryor's Fork—and it is my honest opinion that had it not been for the infantry, who constituted a part of the military command, there would have been another massacre to add to that of Fort [C.F.] Smith and Kearny.

As I have been in every valley tributary to the Yellowstone, I am familiar with the rich alluvial soils, its wealth of grass lands and its mineral possibilities. From 25-Yard creek to the Bad Lands, this great and noble river, dotted with islands ever green with cottonwood groves, swiftly pursues its way to mix its pure waters with the muddy current of the Missouri, ever whispering of romance and tragedy amid silence unbroken, save by the lowing of countless herds of game or the scream of thousands of wolves.

United Confederate Veteran leader Frank D. "Sandbar" Brown. *Montana Historical Society 941-266.*

I have lain in my buffalo robes and looked up at the starlit heavens and whitened crests of lofty enclosing mountains, and wondered why the emigrant should wheel his way to more distant lands to find the home he sought. The Indian alone was the obstacle, and he would finally be removed by the tide of emigration flowing up the Platte and Missouri. And I am grateful to know that I have lived to see the day which I predicted would come, where the trails had given way to the railroad, where the schoolhouse, church, village and city invite you to tarry and abide, where fenced lands destroyed the primeval serenity. Prior's Gap, and the immense area of lowly well watered valleys, within the last 50 years, have given homes to thousands.

Frank Brown told varying stories of how he earned the nickname "Sandbar." At times, the story took place on the Yellowstone River, while other times the incident occurred on the Upper Missouri. Perhaps the most plausible account came when Brown was asked by a newspaperman to explain the peculiar significance of the name:

It was in 1866 with two other men. I was riding along the Missouri, about seven miles above the Marias [River]. One of the men was across a ridge, and my other partner had crossed the river and had disappeared from view. I forded over a long sandbar, got the three horses hidden in some willows and backtracked, as we knew some Indians were following us. Hidden behind some sand, I saw three Bloods [Kainai Blackfoot] following our tracks. They had their guns ready, and you know Bloods never gave a white man a chance. They always killed from ambush. As the first Indian got over to the bar, I fired and he dropped. My partner heard the shot and came running back. I got the second Indian, and my partner got the third. We scalped them and threw their bodies in the river. I guess that's how I got "Sandbar" tacked to my name.

In 1873, Andrew Jackson Davis hired Brown to locate mines in the early days of Butte, and his skill in locating the Lexington and other substantial mines contributed to the early success of both the mining camp and Davis's personal fortune. That same year, Brown married Anna Elizabeth Lentz in Helena. They went on to have eight children.

"Sandbar" Brown moved to Philipsburg in 1878 to join the Northwestern Mining Company. He owned and edited the *Philipsburg Mail* newspaper, and for the next forty years, he managed and developed placer and quartz mines in the area.

Brown attended all Democratic state conventions for four decades, although he never ran for public office. He was a member of the Sons of the American Revolution and served proudly as major general in the United Confederate Veterans, commanding the Northwest Division for Montana, Idaho, Washington, the Dakotas and Wyoming. He was known as a brilliant conversationalist and orator.

An active member of the Society of Montana Pioneers, Brown was elected historian in 1908 and secretary in 1923. He played a key role in locating and promoting monuments to Lieutenant John Mullan and the Mullan Road, the first wagon road from Fort Benton to Fort Walla Walla, Washington Territory. The marble Mullan Monuments begin on the levee in Fort Benton and extend across Montana at key points along the famed Mullan Military Wagon Road.

In his later years, Brown ranched and sold real estate and insurance. At the age of eighty-five, Private Frank D. "Sandbar" Brown, veteran of the Confederate army and marines and major general of the United Confederate Veterans, passed away in Missoula on January 16, 1931. The old Confederate soldier rests today in Philipsburg Cemetery.

Chapter 12

A SLAVE AND HIS CONFEDERATE MASTER GO TO WAR

JOSEPH WELLS

When General Robert E. Lee surrendered his army at Appomattox in April 1865, thirty-six African Americans were listed on the Confederate paroles. Most served as servants, musicians, cooks, teamsters or blacksmiths. Throughout the Civil War, thousands of blacks accompanied Confederate army regiments, though only a handful were accepted as combat soldiers until the last months of the war. The Confederate fighting force was white, but much of its support was black.

One young slave, Joseph Wells, went into the Confederate army early in the war as a "body servant" for his master, Colonel Benjamin G. Wells. He would not have worn "the gray," but on occasion he might have fought alongside his master. Joseph remained in company with his master throughout the war.

Joseph said in an interview years later:

> [Colonel Wells] *was a Confederate soldier, and I went to war with him, waiting on him during his service in the army. He was with General Price. The first place we fought was at Blue Mill Landing. We had a little skirmish there. We had a scrap at Lexington, Missouri, where General Price, with 40,000 men, dislodged 3,000 Union soldiers, but not until he cut off the water supply. We had brushes at Elk Grove and Oak Hill and a battle right at Vicksburg. I went with the old man to Texas, and from there we returned home* [to Buchanan County, Missouri].

The slave who was to become Joseph Wells was born in 1838, the "property" of prominent John Fry of Lexington, Kentucky. His mother was sold shortly after his birth, so another slave woman raised him. When he was ten years old, Mr. Fry took Joseph with the Fry family to live near St. Joseph, Buchanan County, Missouri. The U.S. Census in 1850 recorded fifty-seven-year-old farmer John Fry living in Buchanan County with his wife, Mary; four sons; and one daughter. The 1850 Slave Schedule listed one twelve-year-old black male (Joseph) in the household and some twenty-five other slaves spread around other parts of Missouri.

When John Fry died, his widow married Colonel Benjamin G. Wells in 1856. The U.S. Census of 1860 showed the Wells family owned one twenty-two-year-old male slave in Rushville, Buchanan County. One year later, Colonel Wells and his young slave went off to war. While Missouri did not secede to join the Confederacy, a large segment of the population centered in northern Missouri and Little Dixie along the Missouri River favored secession, and many men joined the Missouri State Guard under General Sterling Price.

In September 1861, the pro-secession state guard was ordered to recruit more troops from northwestern Missouri and concentrate at Lexington. Colonel Wells raised a company in Rush Township in southwestern Buchanan County and, with other recruits, departed to join General Price. Some four thousand state guard troops, including Colonel Wells, passed through Liberty to cross the Missouri River at Blue Mills Landing and proceed eastward to Lexington. A Union force of six hundred men under Lieutenant Colonel John Scott was sent to intercept the state guard troops at Blue Mills Landing but arrived after most of the state guard had already crossed the river. Scott's troops moved to engage the remaining state guard soldiers, including Colonel Wells and his servant, who were positioned in the brush on both sides of the road leading to the landing. In midafternoon on September 17, Colonel Scott's troops marched into the ambush. In the one-hour skirmish that followed, Price's men held the advantage, with eighteen Union soldiers killed and eighty wounded at the cost of just three state guard soldiers killed and eighteen wounded.

With this minor victory at Blue Mill Landing (or Battle of Liberty), the northwest Missouri troops proceeded on to join General Price in Lexington, twenty miles east of Kansas City. The First Battle of Lexington, in which the Missouri State Guard fought a smaller Union garrison of 3,500 men holding the town under Colonel James A. Mulligan, lasted from September 13 to September 20, 1861. Over the next several days, General Price's guard received ammunition wagons, other supplies and reinforcements, including those from Buchanan County.

By the eighteenth, the state guard now numbered more than fifteen thousand men, and General Price ordered an assault on Lexington. The state guard moved forward into the face of heavy artillery fire, pushing Union troops back into their inner defenses. On the morning of the twentieth, Price's men advanced behind mobile breastworks made of dampened hemp, which were immune to Union shells. By early afternoon, Colonel Mulligan's men had stacked their arms and surrendered. Lexington, the Union stronghold, had fallen. The victory bolstered Southern sentiment and briefly consolidated Confederate control of the Missouri Valley.

Further details of the activities of Colonel Wells and his servant, Joseph, during the Civil War are sketchy, though they apparently remained part of the Missouri State Guard. General Price and his men formally joined the Confederate cause in Neosho, Missouri, on October 30, 1861. Despite his early victories in Missouri, General Price could not garner enough popular support to hold the border state in the face of Union determination.

By early 1862, Union forces had pushed Price out of Missouri, and with their defeat at the Battle of Pea Ridge in northwestern Arkansas on March 6–8, Confederate's hopes of occupying Missouri ended. For most of 1862–63, the Missouri State Guard fought small skirmishes in Missouri and major battles in Arkansas and Mississippi. Missouri remained threatened by guerrilla warfare from Southern bushwhacker raids throughout the war.

Although Joseph Wells does not mention whether he and Colonel Wells participated in the Battle of Pea Ridge, he does state that they "had brushes at Elk Grove and Oak Hill and a battle right at Vicksburg." Wells's mention of Oak Hill is intriguing. The first major battle of the Trans-Mississippi was the Battle of Wilson's Creek, fought between Union forces and the Missouri State Guard on August 10, 1861, near Springfield, Missouri. That battle is also known as the Battle of Oak Hills. The battle led to the death of brilliant Union commander Brigadier General Nathaniel Lyon and the retreat of Union forces, resulting in the battle also being called the "Bull Run of the West." Colonel Wells's role, if any, in the battle is not known.

During the decisive Vicksburg Campaign (May 19–July 4, 1863), Missouri infantry and cavalry fought in the First and Second Brigades of Major General John S. Bowen's division of the Confederate army. As General Ulysses S. Grant began to move to capture Vicksburg, General Bowen was assigned a division in General John C. Pemberton's army defending Vicksburg. After uniting with Pemberton's army, General Bowen's division fought at the Battle of Champion Hill, where its counterattack almost split Grant's army in half. When the rest of Pemberton's army failed to support Bowen's attack, his division was forced to retreat. Bowen's division suffered defeat at the Battle of Big Black River Bridge, retreated to Vicksburg and took part in the final defense of that city. The surrender of Vicksburg on July 4, 1863, was a devastating blow to the Confederacy. Not only were 2,872 men killed and wounded and 29,495 taken prisoner, but the Confederacy also strategically lost control of the Mississippi River and was cut in two.

Details about the end of the war and the surrender of Colonel and Joseph Wells are sketchy. Joseph claimed that toward the end of the war, "I went with the old man to Texas, and from there we returned home." In May 1865, Joseph Wells, now a freedman, returned briefly to St. Joseph, Missouri. There, Mrs. Wells, his former mistress, warned him to leave because of his Confederate army service. In turn, Colonel Wells offered Joseph a span of mules worth $500, a wagon and provisions for a year if he would stay and haul timber from the river bottoms. Joseph listened to his mistress.

Like many white Confederate soldiers, Joseph headed west in the early summer of 1865, stopping along the Overland Stage Line near today's Cheyenne, Wyoming, to work as a cook before proceeding on to California. Wells then decided to move on to Denver, Colorado, where he worked odd jobs. From there, he headed north to Alder Gulch, Montana Territory, to try his hand at placer gold mining. With some success, he accumulated $10,000.

By 1870, Joseph Wells was living at Fort Shaw and working as a servant for Brevet Major S.A. Russell, 7th Infantry Regiment, helping care for Russell's four-year-old son, Louis. Six years later, Joseph Wells stampeded to the gold rush in the Black Hills, where he claimed that "Nigger Hill" was named for him.

The Negro Hill district was a section in the western part of the Black Hills that derived its name from a mountain that rose some 6,400 feet above sea level with a summit high above the surrounding peaks of the rugged neighborhood. The steep slopes of Negro Hill form the heads of various gulches—Bear, Mallory, Negro, Sand and Beaver—from which hundreds of thousands of dollars in placer gold were taken.

Negro Hill and Negro Gulch were named for several African Americans, including Joseph Wells, who owned an immensely rich placer claim from which they took a fortune during the summer of 1876. Four of these black miners took out $1,700 in a single day, hauling their gravel hundreds of yards to wash it. Several other black miners built a dam to accumulate water for sluicing and washed out $1,500 in a remarkable half day.

Ex-slave Joseph Wells, pictured here on the streets of Missoula, Montana, with his dog, went to war with his master, Colonel Benjamin Wells. *From the* Opheim (MT) Observer, *January 8, 1923.*

The reputation of these black miners was so colorful that the mountain was named to commemorate them. These were the first placer gold strikes discovered in the northern Black Hills in the summer of 1876, and they led to a stampede to the area. Joseph Wells successfully mined Negro Gulch and accumulated $30,000. Unfortunately, he squandered his riches in just three months, drinking and gambling before moving on to Deadwood, Dakota Territory.

In the early 1880s, Joseph Wells returned to Montana, where he lived in poverty and ill health in Billings. After regaining his strength, he returned to mining placer claims on Williams Creek on the Shoshone Reservation.

In the early 1900s, Joseph Wells arrived in Missoula to become a favorite of local newspaper reporters. In August 1910, the *Missoulian* told "Uncle Joe's" story. Joe claimed an age of 120 years, perhaps identifying in his mind with the actual age of his former master, Colonel Wells. Joe's age at the time was about seventy-two years. Other details of his story ring true and are consistent with facts that can be checked. He told about his early years in slavery, his service in the war with his master and his migration westward. In the interview, the reporter quizzed Wells about his Black Hills experiences:

> *"I went into the Black hills and crossed to Nigger gulch, where I lifted $30,000 inside a month."*
>
> *"What! You took out $30,000 worth of gold?"*
>
> *"Yes, sir, and the gulch was named after me. I had $30,000 in clean cash at one time."*
>
> *"What did you do with it?"*
>
> *"Squandered it," said he, indifferently as he looked down at his frayed trousers. "In them days I did not know the value of money. I drank and gambled my $30,000 away in three months."*
>
> *"Were you not afraid somebody would rob you."*
>
> *"Not a bit. I carried the best of arms and could use them like a man. I went with an English bull [a Bull Dog pocket revolver], a dangerous pistol, up my sleeve all the time."*
>
> *"Where did you keep your money?"*
>
> *"With me. I wore two pairs of pants, one over the other, and had secret pockets. My outer garments were of buckskin."*
>
> *"What sort of gambling did you do?"*
>
> *"Faro. That was the game them days."*
>
> *"How long ago was that?"*
>
> *"Thirty years."*

"Soon after the Nigger gulch find I went to Billings. I was broke, and sick. For two years I lay there in the Sisters' hospital. Every now and then I would tell the nurses that I was burning daylight. As soon as I was able to travel, I secured me a horse—a white one—and went to Copper Mountain. After three weeks of prospecting, I sprung off to Shoshone Reservation and located six claims on Williams Creek. I have them yet. Some fellow tried to get them out of me, but I told him that I was from Missouri."

"What are you doing now?"

"I am on the way to Flathead to prospect. If I get up there, and find anything, I will go to work."

"How do you go about it?"

"I have done my work along. I cut the timber and go in with my wheel-barrow. Give me a bit of giant powder, and I can do the rest. I know how to handle that, boy."

The *Missoulian* reporter opined:

There is no more unique citizen in western Montana than Joe Wells. The general impression among his acquaintances, both white and black, is that he has slipped a cog or two on his age but all agree that he is far beyond the three score and ten milepost. His warped limbs, his wrinkled face, and his white hair indicate that he is close to the century mark. In appearance, he is scrawny and sharp. On his face there stands, at irregular intervals, bunches of whiskers—sagebrush—and on his head a scanty stand of hair. On the point of his little black chin there hangs, like a bit of Florida moss, a tuft of beard done in a three-stand plait. The Missoulian man, when trying to locate him, asked a neighbor if she had seen him. She looked into space, in an effort to recall him, but the moment the twig of whiskers was mentioned, she smiled and said: "He's right there—next door."

Two friends Joe Wells keeps near him: a pocket magnifying glass to help in his search for gold, and Nailer, a big, shaggy dog. With these he roams in search of a fortune. The old fellow's heart is full of hope, and so long as he is able to move, he will hunt for gold. News of strikes at Dixon has reached his ear, and he is eager to get back in harness.

"Oh, but if I could make one more lucky strike," is his song.

If Joe Wells were to step into a Kentucky street, some old-time southern man would greet him: "Good morning, Uncle Joe. How are you?" and he would respond: "Thank you, Marse John; poly thank Gawd." But out here, he is as gay and chipper as a tree frog, and knows all of the up-to-date vernacular. He is as cunning as a fox.

Ten years later, in 1920, Joe Wells was still in Missoula, renting a house with a white barber. In December 1922, Joe Wells died at St. Patrick's Hospital in Missoula. His death was noted with a short obituary and a photograph published by the Montana Newspaper Association in January 1923:

> *Missoula Centenarian Dies. Joseph Wells, colored, once winner of the Kentucky Derby, believed to be the oldest inhabitant in Missoula, died at St. Patrick's hospital a few days ago.*
>
> *"Uncle Joe," as he was best known in the city, claimed to have been born at Louisville, Ky., in 1807, placing his age at 115 years. His mother, a slave in the southern city, was sold shortly after his birth and...[he was] reared by another colored woman. The aged negro often narrated the vicissitudes of his fortune during early slavery times, the stirring days of rebellion and the new era following the Civil War. He made many trips up and down "the ol' Mississippi."*
>
> *His story of once winning the Kentucky Derby as [a black] jockey, strapped to the back of the winner of the blue-grass classic, was one worthy of literary prominence. To have heard old "Uncle Joe" tell it himself in his own mannerisms was still more interesting.*

Oh, to have been able to interview Joseph Wells, learn more details and probe some of his stories. From the first Kentucky Derby in 1875, most derby jockeys were African American. That was until Jim Crow laws ended the practice about 1900. Thirteen of the fifteen riders in the first Kentucky Derby were black jockeys, and about half of the derbies featured blacks. The names of these early day black sports superstars are readily available—sadly, Joseph Wells does not appear among them.

Despite his exaggerations, Joseph Wells, slave, Confederate service soldier, gold miner, servant, rich man, poor man, drinker and carouser and kindly "Uncle Joe" the storyteller, lived more than a full life before passing away in Missoula on December 16, 1922. He is interred in an unmarked grave in Saint Mary Cemetery, Missoula.

Chapter 13

WHEN TRUTH IS STRANGER
THAN FICTION

THE STEAMBOAT *RICHMOND* AND
LANGFORD "FARMER" PEEL

Montana is home to some truly outrageous characters and stories, many growing out of the Civil War era. Some are true, and some stretch the truth. This story may well top them all, and yet there is strong evidence it is grounded in truth. This is the story of Langford "Farmer" Peel and a mysterious trip on the steamboat *Richmond* to the Upper Missouri in the summer of 1867.

This tale involves a weathered old headboard on display at the Montana Historical Society in Helena. The marker came from the grave of an old-timer who met with a violent death in post–Civil War Montana Territory. In the intriguing mix are: Quantrill guerrillas, a battered steamboat, a teenage traveler and a charming killer and his grave marker. For skeptics who read this stranger-than-fiction story, the source is unimpeachable: Charles N. Pray, three times Montana congressman (1907–13) and federal court judge for over three decades. Pray learned the story from his father-in-law, Hans J. Wackerlin, a seventeen-year-old traveler on the steamboat who became a respected merchant in Fort Benton.

The headboard is splintered, cracked, worn and gray with age. On it is an inscription, now barely legible, that reads:

Sacred to the Memory of Langford Peel
Born in Liverpool
Died July 23d, 1867
Aged 36 Years

Young Hans Wackerlin learned the story of Farmer Peel on his trip up the Missouri River aboard the *Richmond*. *Overholser Historical Research Center.*

In life beloved by his friends, and Respected by his enemies.
Vengeance is Mine, sayeth the Lord.
I know that my Redeemer liveth.
Erected by a Friend

The epitaph begs the questions: Who was Langford Peel? What was happening in Montana Territory at this time? And why was he here? The year 1867 was a pivotal one in the new territory, still in its formative gold rush years, with heavy postwar migration triggering a growing Indian War. This was rugged frontier country. It was a time when General Thomas Francis Meagher, hero of the Irish Brigade and acting governor of Montana Territory, mysteriously disappeared off a steamboat at the Fort Benton levee. It was a time when the head of navigation, Fort Benton, earned a reputation as the "Bloodiest Block in the West" and when characters like Eleanor DuMont, "Madame Moustache," infamous gambler and madam, played blackjack at a corner table and served booze and girls to all takers.

Montana Territory at this time was filled with men, women and children who had lived through the war, including many soldiers who had served the Confederacy in the army of General Price, William Quantrill and "Bloody Bill" Anderson. Among these desperadoes who had never accepted the defeat in the Civil War was a group led by Langford M. Peel. At the end of the war, Peel and his men headed west to fight for Mexican emperor Maximilian. By the time they got there, Maximilian had been executed, so the outlaw gang drifted back into lawless postwar Texas. Peel abruptly left his gang, and his men concluded that in addition to having stolen their "stolen" money, he had also tried to betray them to federal authorities.

So who was Langford Peel? Born in Belfast, Ireland, in 1829, Peel immigrated to the United States with his mother and stepfather. In 1841, Peel, at just twelve years of age, enlisted as a bugler in the band of the 1st New York Dragoons. In 1847, Bugler Peel rode with Company B to Santa Fe. His company engaged a band of Comanche at Coon Creek, Kansas, where Peel killed two Comanches. Peel remained in the army, and at age nineteen, his first sergeant described him as a perfect specimen of a soldier, saying Peel was "a perfect horseman, possessing unlimited courage and endurance."

In January 1848, Peel's 1st Dragoons, under General Sterling Price and the Army of the West, invaded Mexico and fought in the Battle of Santa Cruz de Rosales in the state of Chihuahua. When the war with Mexico ended, Peel reenlisted in the army and was promoted to sergeant. His army career ended abruptly due to some unknown trouble with his discharge in 1855 "by Civil Authority."

It was at this point in time that Peel began a downward spiral into a life of crime and violence. He moved his family to Leavenworth City, Kansas, where he soon fell into the life of a gambler and gained the nickname "Farmer" Peel for reasons unknown. He also gained a reputation for being both generous to the needy and quick on the trigger. Leaving his wife and son, he drifted around the West, going from Leavenworth to Salt Lake to Los Angeles, and acquired a reputation for gambling and killing.

At the outbreak of the Civil War, Peel apparently returned to Missouri and served with guerrilla groups in General Price's army, although details of his war service are scarce. As the war ended, a group of Quantrill's guerrillas went south of the border to fight for Maximilian, then emperor of Mexico. This group, led by Langford Peel, arrived about the time Maximilian was captured and executed.

Peel and his soldiers of fortune returned to the United States, settling in Texas, where they drifted into lawless pursuits. The band was large and proved too unwieldy for Peel to control. In a short time, strife arose within their ranks, and Peel made off with all their spoils, which should have been equally divided. Worse than that, his gang believed he had conspired to have them captured by federal and state authorities. Survivors of the band soon learned that Peel had gone up the Missouri River and was spending their money in the saloons of Montana Territory. The gang swore to track Peel down and avenge his treachery.

To follow Peel, the gang concocted an amazing scheme. On the Red River, which flows from Texas down through Louisiana, they discovered a light-draft steamboat, the *Richmond*. This they commandeered one night at its moorings and then pressed African American firemen and deckhands into service. The gang's leader was an experienced steamboat man, Captain A.B. Miller, so he got the boilers steamed up, and the steamer proceeded downriver toward the Gulf of Mexico.

Handling freight along the way to meet expenses, the *Richmond* landed at St. Louis. There, the men loaded 270 tons of cargo and twenty-five passengers and set out on May 8 to steam up the Missouri River to Fort Benton. The voyage of the *Richmond* was one wild ride. At the river port of St. Joseph, Missouri, seven more passengers boarded, including seventeen-year-old Hans. J. Wackerlin, bound for an adventurous life on the Upper Missouri.

Young Wackerlin's impeccable marksmanship and demeanor quickly impressed Captain Miller and his men, who made something of a pet of him. Over time, Wackerlin learned the story of the hard-bitten crew and their secret mission. As he became better acquainted with members of the *Richmond*'s crew, Wackerlin learned their history and became conscious of the fact that he was in the midst of one of the most notorious of Quantrill's outlaw bands. At each landing where the boat stopped, most of the crew would go ashore to blow off steam. But hard drinkers and lawless as they were, they never attempted to harm young Wackerlin. Rather, they treated him in a friendly, considerate manner. He said that sober, they were a strange, picturesque lot, possessing rough humor to temper the evil of their ways. Under the influence of liquor, however, they were brutal and quarrelsome. One time, after much abuse, they drove all the black deckhands overboard.

After this incident, the *Richmond* docked at a small town where a traveling minstrel troupe was giving a performance for the entertainment of the settlement. Captain Miller induced the troupe to take passage on the *Richmond* upriver. After the boat was cast loose, these entertainers found themselves pressed into service as deckhands, roles they continued throughout the remainder of the trip. At night, they entertained the guerrillas and passengers with music and recitations.

Adventurous as the journey proved to be, the Quantrill men did not for a moment forget the main purpose of their expedition. As they neared Fort Benton, their longing for revenge against Peel was uppermost in their minds and conversation. Within their own circles, they discussed the treatment Peel would receive after they had discovered him—and it was brutal.

Meanwhile, after terrorizing Virginia City, Nevada, and killing six men there, Farmer Peel left for Helena, Montana, with his partner, John E. Bull. Peel and Bull had a stormy relationship as they dabbled in mining and spent their evenings in saloons. On the night of July 23, after another falling-out with Peel that culminated in having his face slapped, Bull stormed out of Headly & Chase's Saloon. Some hours later, around midnight, Bull ambushed Peel as he departed the saloon with Bell Neil on his arm and shot him down.

A reporter for the *Montana Post* described the killing, writing that as Peel saw Bull, he drew his revolver, but not quickly enough. Bull fired three shots, the first going through Peel's heart and proving fatal. The second shot entered his left side and the third his left cheek, the pistol being held so close that his cheek was burned. Peel fell from the first shot and never got off a round. Evidently, judging from the shots fired after Peel fell, Bull was not willing to take any chances that Peel was still alive. Bull was tried for murder, but a jury, after deliberating for just one hour, found him "not guilty," to the ringing cheers of his friends.

Arriving at the mouth of the Judith River, ninety-one miles downriver from Fort Benton, the *Richmond* tied up and a scout was dispatched overland to Fort Benton to learn if Peel was there and, if not, where he had gone. In less than a week, the scout returned with the news that Peel had been killed in a gambling house fight at Helena only a few days prior to their arrival.

The Quantrill men held a conference and decided to proceed to Fort Benton to off-load cargo and passengers and confirm the report of Peel's killing. Arriving at Fort Benton on July 28, they received confirmation of the report, but they dispatched a party to Helena to make sure that Peel was, indeed, dead and buried and to try to locate the stolen loot. The crew then cut loose on one of the biggest sprees ever seen by Madame Moustache and the other gamblers and adventurers conducting business along the Bloodiest Block in the West.

With their mission accomplished, the crew boarded the *Richmond* and departed Fort Benton. By the time the steamer arrived at Sioux City, federal

No known photograph of the renegade steamboat *Richmond* exists. This photo of the *DeSmet* was taken at Fort Benton in 1868. *Overholser Historical Research Center.*

authorities were on their trail. The gang abandoned the *Richmond* and struck out overland for Idaho. There, they lived the lives of road agents for a time, some of their number being killed. Others went to Cheyenne and opened up a gambling house. Captain Miller finally went to Quantrill's ranch in Texas, where he later died of tuberculosis.

As for Farmer Peel, he was buried in the old graveyard just to the west of Helena High School. A plank of wood marked the grave, the headboard now in possession of the Montana Historical Society. The *Montana Post* eulogized Peel: "He was a man of many generous impulses, princely in his dealings with his friends, and to his enemies implacable. Altogether he was one whom few cared to have any dealings with and he was shunned by his own associates, as such men usually are."

Peel might have been shunned by his associates, as the *Post* asserted, yet that memorial marker from his grave is proof that despite being a serial killer and all-round bad man, at least one person cared enough for him to mark his last resting place.

As for young Hans Wackerlin, he became one of Fort Benton's most highly respected pioneer businessmen, operating Wackerlin's Hardware for

Wooden grave marker for Quantrill Raider Langford "Farmer" Peel. *Montana Historical Society 944-309*.

many years, with T.C. Power backing. His future son-in-law, Charles N. Pray, absolutely believed this amazing tale and told it often.

Note: Guerrilla leader William Quantrill's younger brother Thompson also lived for a time in Montana Territory in the 1880s. Thompson, described as a vile, worthless, despicable scoundrel, enlisted in the U.S. 14th Infantry Regiment in August 1870 and deserted one month later.

Chapter 14

THE PERSISTENCE OF THE "LOST CAUSE"

After four long years of war, on April 9, 1865, at Appomattox, Generals Ulysses S. Grant and Robert E. Lee met to sign an agreement surrendering the Army of Northern Virginia, effectively ending the war. For General Grant, the Union victory stemmed from the righteous virtue of its cause and the valor of its men. But for General Lee, the question was: What will history say? A new campaign had begun, not on the battlefield but rather for the hearts and minds of the reuniting nation. On April 10, 1865, General Lee fired his opening salvo with his farewell (General Order No. 9) to his officers and men. The general wrote:

> *After four years of arduous service, marked by unsurpassed courage and fortitude, the Army of Northern Virginia has been compelled to yield to overwhelming numbers and resources. I need not tell the brave survivors of so many hard-fought battles, who have remained steadfast to the last, that I have consented to this result from no distrust of them. But feeling that valor and devotion could accomplish nothing that would compensate for the loss that must have attended the continuance of the contest, I determined to avoid the useless sacrifice of those whose past services have endeared them to their countrymen.*
>
> *By the terms of the agreement, officers and men can return to their homes and remain until exchanged. You will take with you the satisfaction that proceeds from the consciousness of duty faithfully performed; and I earnestly pray that a merciful God will extend to you his blessing and protection.*

Generals U.S. Grant and Robert E. Lee at Appomattox, April 9, 1865. *United Confederate Veteran Convention 1895; Author's collection.*

Opposite: General Robert E. Lee's General Order No. 9 farewell. *United Confederate Veteran Convention 1895; Author's collection.*

FINIS

HEAD QUARTERS, A.N.V.

APRIL 10th 1865

General Order No 9.

After four years of arduous service, marked by unsurpassed courage and fortitude, the Army of Northern Virginia has been compelled to yield to overwhelming numbers and resources.

I need not tell the brave survivors of so many hard fought battles, who have remained steadfast to the last, that I have consented to this result from no distrust of them. But feeling that valor and devotion could accomplish nothing that would compensate for the loss that must have attended the continuation of the contest I determined to avoid the sacrifice of those whose past services have endeared them to their countrymen.

By the terms of agreement officers and men can return to their homes and remain until exchanged.

You will take with you the satisfaction that proceeds from the consciousness of duty faithfully performed; and I earnestly pray that a merciful God will extend to you His blessing and protection.

With an unceasing admiration of your constancy and devotion to your country, and a grateful remembrance of your kind and generous consideration of myself, I bid you an affectionate farewell.

R.E. Lee, General.

With an increasing admiration of your constancy and devotion to your country and a grateful remembrance of your kind and generous considerations for myself, I bid you an affectionate farewell.

R.E. Lee, General

As he rode among his exhausted and starving soldiers, Lee echoed his theme: "The odds against us were too great." His farewell address and his consoling words had a profound impact on both his men and white Southerners. For Confederates, the battle themes were: "The Union victory was one of might over right" and "The South was right to fight."

Even before the end of the war, Southern women were transforming their wartime soldiers and associations into memorials for their "Lost Cause" in the public memory. Within a year after the end of the Civil War, the myth of the Lost Cause had become firmly engrained. Edward A. Pollard, wartime editor of the *Richmond Examiner*, placed the term "Lost Cause" on a pedestal in 1866 when he published *The Lost Cause: A New Southern History of the War of the Confederates*.

The Lost Cause was further developed by General Robert E. Lee, Confederate president Jefferson Davis, the United Confederate Veterans, the United Daughters of the Confederacy and other white Southerners (including many former Confederate generals) who sought to present the war in the best possible terms for the Confederacy. Dwelling on the postwar climate of political, economic and racial uncertainty, the Lost Cause romanticized the "Old South" and the Confederate war effort and tended to ignore the "peculiar institution" of slavery. Having lost the war, the South was determined to win the peace on its terms. The myth of the Lost Cause provided a sense of relief to white Southerners concerned about dishonor in their defeat, and many white northern Americans found it an attractive way to ease the South back into the Union.

Reconstruction collapsed throughout the South just one decade after the war, and Jim Crow laws began to institutionalize segregation and discrimination. Some African Americans migrated to Montana and elsewhere in the West to seek safer and more open societies. What they found was a milder but still pervasive form of discrimination that would not break down until the civil rights movement of the 1950s and '60s.

On May 30, 1901, a Soldiers Monument was dedicated in Soldiers Plot in Highland Cemetery at Great Falls. This monument was the first monument in the nation to honor both the Blue and the Gray.

Cover of *The United Daughters of the Confederacy Magazine. Author's collection.*

Above: Soldiers Monument at Highland Cemetery, Great Falls, Montana—the first tribute in the nation to both the Rebel and Yankee soldiers. *Author's photo*.

Left: Monument panel honoring Confederate soldiers: "In Memory of the Boys Who Wore the Gray 1861–1865." *Author's photo*.

Helena's Confederate Memorial, once the northernmost monument to the Confederacy in the United States. *Author's collection.*

The dedication in Helena, Montana's capital, in 1916 of a Confederate monument was symptomatic of the lingering myth of the Lost Cause far beyond the South. On Helena's Hill Park stands the Confederate Memorial Fountain, erected by the Daughters of the Confederacy. Its inscription reads, "A Loving Tribute to Our Confederate Soldiers."

Nostalgia for the "Old South" influenced popular entertainment such as minstrel shows for many decades. Other entertainment, such as books like *The Klansmen* and movies like *Birth of a Nation*, continued the powerful myth.

The veteran organization United Confederate Veterans (UCV) became active in Montana in the mid-1890s. In 1902, two Montanans—Northwest Division commander Major General Frank D. Brown and Montana Brigade commander Brigadier General Paul A. Fusz, both of Philipsburg—attended the national Twelfth Annual Meeting and Reunion of the UCV in Dallas, Texas.

United Confederate Veteran Camps
Montana Brigade

Robert E. Lee No. 1,379	Butte
General Marmaduke No. 1,384	Livingston
Stonewall Jackson No. 1,385	Townsend
General Parsons No. 1,386	Twin Bridges
Nathan Bedford Forrest No. 1,390	Helena
Jefferson Davis No. 523	Great Falls
J.B. Stuart No. 716	Philipsburg
Emmett McDonald No. 1,370	Missoula
Joe Shelby No. 1,371	Hamilton
Roger Hanson No. 1,377	Anaconda
Sterling Price No. 1,378	Bozeman

Typical of the annual reunions was the fifth annual reunion of the UCV of the Northwest Division, held at Townsend on October 11–12, 1906. Among the old soldiers of the South serving as delegates from Montana were: J.C. Woolverton, Livingston; Paul A. Fusz, G.W. Crosswhite and J.H. Williams, Philipsburg; Shirley C. Ashby and George F. Ingram, Helena; Reverend Davis B. Price, Stevensville; Dr. James L. Belcher, Robert Fields, William G. Boone, Joseph Wine, Albert Wells, A.P. Pue and J.W. Henton, Townsend; and the General Sterling Price Camp from Bozeman, which had the largest delegation present (headed by William H.H. Ellis, brigadier general of the Montana Brigade, members also included C.P. Blakeley, White Calfee, David Marshall, L.T. Tillery and F.W. Webster—William H. Mayo of St. Louis, temporarily residing in Bozeman, was passed into service by General Ellis and adopted by the camp). Many members of the United Daughters of the Confederacy were present as well. Headed by Mrs. J.L. Patterson of Bozeman, other members included Miss Eva Morris, Helena, and Mrs. James L. Belcher, Townsend.

As each delegation arrived, they were escorted to the palatial residence of Dr. James L. Belcher, which was at once declared to be "headquarters" during the convention. There, the scar-worn, grisly old veterans met the daughters and were cheered and rejuvenated by sweet entrancing music, the singing of old familiar southern songs and the recital of camp, march and battle incidents and hairbreadth escapades.

During the afternoon of the eleventh, the Northwest Division and the Montana Brigade held their business sessions in the auditorium, which had been beautifully decorated with U.S. and Confederate flags, bunting, potted plants and evergreens. Paul A. Fusz, of Philipsburg, was reelected major general commanding, and William Ellis, of Bozeman, was reelected commander of the Montana Brigade, both without opposition. But when it came to selecting the place for the reunion the following year, there was a spirited contest. The Helena delegation thought it had a sure thing, but after its presentation and invitation had been heard, General Ellis, on behalf of the General Price Camp, extended the invitation to hold next year's reunion in Bozeman. Mr. Mayo, on behalf of the Mayor and Commercial Club, also made extended remarks emphasizing the beautiful surroundings and the hospitality of Bozeman. When the vote was taken, a large majority favored Bozeman.

That evening, a reception, entertainment and banquet were held. First came music, with singing of nostalgic southern songs by a chorus of young men and women. Mrs. Patterson, of Bozeman, sang the old Confederate marching song "Bonnie Blue Flag" to great applause. A speech of welcome by Dr. Belcher brought a response by General Fusz and William Mayo. A fine banquet followed the music with rations that tickled the palate and gladdened the hearts of old soldiers. The long table was laden with roast pigs, sweet potatoes, crackling corn bread, chickens, roast beef, vegetables, pumpkin pie, cake and coffee. George Ingram, of Helena, served as toastmaster. Captain Joseph Wine responded for Camp Stonewall Jackson, while Reverend D.B. Price spoke about education and progress. William Mayo responded for the ladies of Montana and then told some incidents depicting camp life and stirring war scenes.

We began with the question: What role did Confederates and their sympathizers play in settling Montana Territory? The answer is that Confederates came early in large numbers to the new territory, especially from Missouri and other border states, and many became actively engaged in politics and business. That influence faded over the decades but remained strong enough that a monument to Confederate soldiers was dedicated in 1916.

Montana Territory was forged on battlefields in the eastern and western theaters of the Civil War. Streaming to the Montana gold fields were survivors of the war—those who had seen combat and survived, fled the field of battle or chose to avoid service. As the tide turned against the Confederacy in Missouri and other border states, many came up the Missouri River or overland to salvage their lives and fortunes. Confederate soldiers and sympathizers and their families became a powerful force in the newly formed Montana Territory.

I WISH I WAS IN DIXIE'S LAND.

BY DAN D. EMMETT.

I wish I was in de land ob cotton,
Old times dar am not forgotten,
   Look away, look away, look away, Dixie Land!
In Dixie land whar I was born in,
Early on one frosty mornin',
   Look away, look away, look away, Dixie Land!

Chorus.—Den I wish I was in Dixie—
          Hooray, hooray!
      In Dixie land I'll took my stan'!
      To lib an' die in Dixie
          Away, away,
     Away down south in Dixie.
          Away, away,
     Away down south in Dixie.

Ole Missus marry "Will-de-Weaber,"
William was a gay deceber
   Look away, etc.
But when he put his arm around 'er
He smiled as fierce as a forty-pounder
   Look away, etc.   —Chorus.

His face was sharp as a butcher's cleaber,
But dat did not seem to grieb 'er,
   Look away, etc.
Ole Missus acted de foolish part,
An' died for a man dat broke her heart,
   Look away, etc.   —Chorus.

Dixie Land Tribute. *United Confederate Veteran Convention 1895; author's collection.*

The end of the war brought many more to the territory, from South and North, each with their own scars and memories of the war. For decades to come, the Civil War remained in the minds and hearts of men, women and children, black and white, as they came to frontier Montana. Through veterans' organizations and celebrations of Decoration Day, the war and its casualties were remembered. Homesteaders, land grant college students and descendants of emancipated slaves celebrated the political successes of the war—and all Montanans shared in these. Today, 150 years and many generations later, our united nation and Montana commemorate the Civil War and the profound changes it brought to the lives of us all.

BIBLIOGRAPHY

ONLINE RESOURCES

Ancestry.com

Army and Navy Civil War Service, Enlistment, and Pension Records

Chronicling America

Fold 3 Civil War Records

Frontier Scout

U.S. Census Bureau. Eleventh Census of the United States, 1890. Schedules Enumerating Union Veterans and Widows of Union Veterans and Widows of Union Veterans of the Civil War. Montana Bundle 96. Microfilm, National Archives, Washington, D.C., 1948. (While this is a listing of Union veterans, many Montana Confederate veterans are also recorded with their names crossed out.)

U.S. Census Records

Wikipedia

INTRODUCTION

Robison, Ken. *Montana Territory and the Civil War: A Frontier Forged on the Battlefield*. Charleston, SC: The History Press, 2013.

CHAPTER 1

Albright, R.E. "The American Civil War as a Factor in Montana Territorial Politics." *Pacific Historical Review* 6 (March 1937): 36–46.

Athearn, Robert G. "The Civil War and Montana Gold." Civil War in the West issue. *Montana the Magazine of Western History* 12 (April 1962): 62–73.

———. "West of Appomattox." *Montana the Magazine of Western History* 12 (April 1962): 2–11.

Brown, Kenny L. "Dakota and Montana Territories I: The Western Territories in the Civil War." *Journal of the West* 16 (April 1977): 10–25.

Butte Inter Mountain. "Thousands of Boys Who Fought under the Bonnie Blue Flag Came West When the Awful Struggle Was Over and Established Themselves in What Was Then Truly the Wilderness." January 1, 1903.

Butts, Michele Tucker. *Galvanized Yankees on the Upper Missouri: The Face of Loyalty*. Boulder: University Press of Colorado, 2002.

Chaky, Doreen. *Terrible Justice Sioux Chiefs and U.S. Soldiers on the Upper Missouri, 1854–1868*. Norman, OK: Arthur H. Clark Company, 2012.

Davidson, Stanley R., and Dale Tash. "Confederate Backwash in Montana Territory." *Montana the Magazine of Western History* 17 (October 1967): 50–58.

Etulain, Richard W. "Abraham Lincoln: Political Founding Father of the American West." *Montana the Magazine of Western History* 59 (Summer 2009): 3–22.

Frontier Scout. "A Misrepresentation Corrected." June 15 and 22, 1865.

National Register of Historic Places. The Masonic Temple Building (2 E Main Street/14 S. Tracy Avenue), Bozeman, Montana.

Smurr, J.W., ed. "Jim Crow Out West. In *Historical Essays on Montana and the Northwest.* Helena, MT: Western Press, 1957, 149–203.

Thane, James L., Jr. "The Myth of Confederate Sentiment in Montana." *Montana the Magazine of Western History* 17 (April 1967): 14–19.

CHAPTER 2

"Affairs at Fort Benton, from 1831 to 1869. From Lieut. Bradley's Journal." *Contributions to the Historical Society of Montana* 3 (1900): 201–87.

Cut Bank Pioneer Press. "Pioneer Is Summoned. Henry A. Kennerly, Who Helped Make Early History, Is Dead." July 11, 1913.

Fort Benton River Press. April 24, 2014.

Leeson, Michael A. *History of Montana, 1739–1885.* Chicago: Warner, Beers & Co., 1885, 1015–16.

National Archives. *Compiled Service Records of Confederate Soldiers Who Served in Organizations from the State of Missouri.*

Walter, David A., ed. "The 1855 Blackfeet Treaty Council: A Memoir by Henry A. Kennerly." *Montana the Magazine of Western History* 32 (Winter 1982): 44–51.

CHAPTER 3

Grass Range Review. February 18, 1924.

Howard, Joseph Kinsey. *Montana: High, Wide, and Handsome*. New Haven, CT: Yale University Press, 1959, 40–41.

Robison, Ken. *Montana Territory and the Civil War: A Frontier Forged on the Battlefield*. Charleston, SC: The History Press, 2013, 33.

Sanders, James U., comp. "Members and Officers of the Legislative Assemblies of the Territory of Montana." *Contributions to the Historical Society of Montana*. Vols. II, III and V. Helena, MT: Rocky Mountain Publishing Co., 1903.

Shelby Tribune. July 25, 1927.

Spence, Clark C. *Territorial Politics and Government in Montana, 1864–89*. Urbana: University of Illinois, 1875, 20–34.

Waldron, Ellis. *An Atlas of Montana Politics Since 1864*. Missoula: Montana State University Press, 1958.

CHAPTER 4

Anaconda Standard. December 10, 1911.

Fort Benton River Press. May 28, 2014.

Lacey, Richard H. *The Montana Militia: A History of Montana's Volunteer Forces, 1867–1976*. Dillon, MT: *Dillon Tribune-Examiner Press*, 1976.

Meagher County News. January 16, 1897.

Montana Post. 1866–68.

Perry, Leslie J. "Appeals to Lincoln's Clemency." *Century Magazine* (December 1895): 252.

Spence, Clark C. *Territorial Politics and Government in Montana, 1864–89.* Urbana: University of Illinois Press, 1976.

Stewart, A.J.D. *The History of the Bench and Bar of Missouri.* St. Louis: Legal Publishing Company, 1898, 331–33.

St. Louis Republic. December 25, 1896.

Thoroughman, Dick. Letter to author. April 17, 2014.

Waldron, Ellis. *An Atlas of Montana Politics Since 1864.* Missoula: Montana State University Press, 1958.

CHAPTER 5

Anaconda Standard. "His Career Sketched: Incidents in the Life of a Man Who Had Much to Live For." December 7, 1897.

———. "Newspaper Writers from an Editorial Sanctum to a Dignified Judicial Position." March 3, 1896.

Ballard, Michael B. *Civil War Mississippi: A Guide.* Jackson: University Press of Mississippi, 2000.

Benton Record. "Changes in the Record." June 9, 1880.

Foster, Gaines M. *Ghosts of the Confederacy: Defeat, the Lost Cause, and the Emergence of the New South.* New York: Oxford University Press, 1987.

Hunt, William H. "A Tribute to Horace R. Buck." *Anaconda Standard,* December 19, 1897.

Warren, Andrea. *Under Siege!: Three Children at the Civil War Battle for Vicksburg.* New York: Farrar Straus Giroux, 2009.

Werner, Emmy E. *Reluctant Witnesses: Children's Voices from the Civil War.* Boulder, CO: Westview Press, 1998.

CHAPTER 6

Benton Record. April 2, 1880; July 21, 1881; January 12, 1882.

Fort Benton River Press. April 27, 1881; August 2, 2006; October 3, 2012.

Great Falls Leader. November 27, 1888; May 25, 1907.

Great Falls Tribune. May 7, 1890; May 23, 1907; July 25, 2012; August 1, 2012; August 29, 2012; May 25, 1907.

Hurst, Jack. *Men of Fire: Grant, Forrest and the Campaign That Decided the Civil War.* New York: Basic Books, 2007.

———. *Nathan Bedford Forrest: A Biography.* New York: Alfred A. Knopf, 1993.

Lilly, John C. "Handwritten Account of John C. Lilly." Overholser Historical Research Center, Fort Benton, MT.

———. Vertical file. Overholser Historical Research Center, Fort Benton, MT.

Wahlberg, Donna. *So Be It: A History of the Barker Mining District Hughesville and Barker, Montana.* N.p.: D. Wahlberg, 1989.

Wyeth, John A. *That Devil Forrest: Life of General Nathan Bedford Forrest.* Baton Rouge: Louisiana State University Press, 1989.

CHAPTER 7

City of Round Rock, Texas. "The Story of Sam Bass." http://www. roundrocktexas.gov/home/index.asp?page=1768.

Fort Benton River Press. November 28, 2012; December 26, 2012; January 2, 2013.

Harris, John F. "Historical Sketch of James F. Berry (1838–1877)." Overholser Historical Research Center, Fort Benton, MT.

Jefferson City (MO) State Journal. October 19, 1877.

Legends of America. "James Berry: A Little Known Outlaw from Missouri." http://www.legendsofamerica.com/we-jamesberry.html.

Miller, Rick. *Sam Bass & Gang.* Austin, TX: State House Press, 1999.

Patterson, William H., comp. "John Harris and Addie Berry Harris Family." Overholser Historical Research Center, Fort Benton, MT.

Pennington's. "Roster of Quantrill's, Anderson's and Todd's Guerrillas and Other 'Missouri Jewels.'" http://penningtons.tripod.com/roster.htm.

Reed, Paula, and Grover Ted Tate. *The Tenderfoot Bandits: Sam Bass and Joel Collins, Their Lives and Hard Times.* Tucson, AZ: Westernlore Press, 1988.

Sedalia Weekly Bazoo. October 23, 1877.

Spring, Agnes Wright. *The Cheyenne and Black Hills Stage and Express Routes.* Glendale, CA: Arthur H. Clark Company, 1949, 192, 226.

CHAPTER 8

Anaconda Standard. July 19 1894.

Conrad, Campbell, and Stanford Family Papers. K. Ross Toole Archives. Maureen and Mike Mansfield Library, University of Montana, Missoula.

Great Falls Tribune. July 18, 1894.

Murphy, James E. *Half Interest in a Silver Dollar: The Saga of Charles E. Conrad.* Missoula, MT: Mountain Press Publishing Company, 1983.

Progressive Men of the State of Montana. Chicago: A.W. Bowen & Co., 1903, 48–50, 904–05.

Siepel, Kevin H. *The Life and Times of John Singleton Mosby.* Lincoln: University of Nebraska Press, 2008.

Wert, Jeffry D. *Mosby's Rangers: The True Adventure of the Most Famous Command of the Civil War.* New York: Simon & Schuster, 1990.

CHAPTER 9

FamilySearch.org. "1st Northeast Regiment, Missouri Calvary (Confederate)." https://familysearch.org/learn/wiki/en/1st_Northeast_Regiment,_Missouri_Cavalry_(Confederate).

———. "9th Regiment, Kentucky Mounted Infantry (Confederate)." http://familysearch.org/learn/wiki/en/9th_Regiment,_Kentucky_Mounted_Infantry_(Confederate).

Flynn, Kelly. *Goldpans, Guns & Grit Diamond City from Territorial Gold Rush to Montana Ghost Town.* Townsend, MT: 2006.

Fort Benton *River Press,* October 30, 2013; November 27, 2013.

Harlowton Women's Club, comp. *Yesteryears and Pioneers*. Harlowton, MT: 1972, 184–85.

"John T. Moore Memoirs." Montana Newspaper Association, *Judith Gap Journal*, July 19, 1926.

Leeson, Michael A. *History of Montana, 1739–1885*. Chicago: Warner, Beers & Co., 1885, 1289.

Meagher County: An Early-Day Pictorial History, 1867–1967. White Sulphur Springs, MT: Meagher County News, 1968, 61.

Progressive Men of Montana. Chicago: A.W. Bowen & Co., circa 1903, 1397–99.

Stout, Tom. *History of Montana*. Vol III. Chicago: American Historical Society, 1921. 1220–21.

CHAPTER 10

Ashby, Colonel Shirley C. "Story as Told by Col. S.C. Ashby." Montana Historical Society, St. Helena. Small Collection 283.

Ashby, Norma. "Ashby Mansion in Helena." *Distinctly Montana* (Winter 2009).

Ashby vertical file. Overholser Historical Research Center, Fort Benton, MT.

Harlowton (MT) News. May 23, 1913.

Helena Record-Herald. July 12, 1939.

Leeson, Michael A. *History of Montana, 1739–1885*. Chicago: Warner, Beers & Co., 1885, 1191.

Miller, Joaquim. *An Illustrated History of the State of Montana*. Chicago: Lewis Publishing Company, 1894, 570–72.

CHAPTER 11

Cooney, Byron E. "'Sandbar' Brown Got His Nickname When He Killed Two Piegan Indians in '72." *Cutbank Pioneer Press*, August 20, 1928.

Cooney, E.H. "How Secretary of Pioneers Became 'Sandbar' Brown. Undated *Fairfield Times* vertical file. Montana Historical Society, St. Helena.

Deer Lodge (MT) Silver State Post. January 22, 1931.

Great Falls Tribune. January 17, 1931.

Helena Record-Herald. "'Sandbar' Brown." January 20, 1930.

Progressive Men of Montana. Chicago: A.W. Bowen & Co., 1903, 1503–04.

CHAPTER 12

Baldwin, George P., ed. *Black Hills Illustrated.* Deadwood, SD: Dakota Graphics, 1904.

Billings Gazette. March 14, 1902.

Fort Benton River Press. February 26, 2014.

Missoulian. August 14, 1910; February 7, 1912; January 29, 1914.

Opheim (MT) Observer. "Missoula Centenarian Dies." January 8, 1923.

Parker, Watson. *Gold in the Black Hills.* Norman: University of Oklahoma Press, 1966, 100.

Yellowstone Journal. July 16, 1884; April 30, 1885.

CHAPTER 13

Conway, Dan R. "Along the River Trail: When Quantrill's Men Steamed up the Missouri River on Their Journey of Revenge Against Farmer Peel." *Mountaineer*, April 11, 1927.

Davis, Sam P., ed. *The History of Nevada*. Vol. 1. Reno, NV: Elms Publishing Co., 1913.

Fort Benton River Press. June 29, 1960.

Great Falls Tribune. April 30, 1922.

Helena Independent. May 13 1874; January 19, 1882; July 23, 1882.

Langford, Nathaniel Pitt. *Vigilantes Days and Ways*. Vol. 1. New York: D.D. Merrill Company, 1893, 270–87.

Montana Post. August 3 and 24, 1867.

Overholser, Joel. *Fort Benton: World's Innermost Port*. Helena, MT: Falcon Press Publishing Co., 1987, 63, 28283.

Philipsburg (MT) Mail. January 13, 1938.

Plassmann, Mrs. M.E. "Gruesome Mementoes of Early Day Outlaws in Historical Library." *Terry Tribune*, September 10, 1928.

CHAPTER 14

Bozeman Chronicle. "Soldiers of the South Have Reunion." October 17, 1906.

Varon, Elizabeth R. *Appomattox: Victory, Defeat, and Freedom at the End of the Civil War*. New York: Oxford University Press, 2014.

INDEX

ABOUT THE AUTHOR

K en Robison is an author and historian who lives in Great Falls, Montana, with his wife, Michele. Ken, a Montana native, is historian at the Overholser Historical Research Center in Fort Benton. He also serves as historian for the Great Falls/Cascade County Historic Preservation Commission and is active in historic preservation throughout Montana. Ken writes monthly columns on Montana's Civil War veterans for two newspapers. His books include: *Montana Territory and the Civil War: A Frontier Forged on the Battlefield; Life and Death on the Upper Missouri: The Frontier Sketches of Johnny Healy; Cascade County and Great Falls;* and *Fort Benton.* He writes historical articles for *Montana the Magazine of Western History* and other regional journals. He is a retired U.S. navy captain after a career in Naval Intelligence. The Montana Historical Society honored Ken as a "Montana Heritage Keeper" in 2010.

www.ingramcontent.com/pod-product-compliance
Lightning Source LLC
Chambersburg PA
CBHW051211090426
42740CB00022B/3458